THE

Language

OF

TAROT

About the Author

Jeannie Reed (New York, NY) has been a tarot master and professional psychic for more than three decades. She designed a scientific system of tarot reading and has been teaching it for twenty-five years. Jeannie has written about oracles for AntiquityNow.org, and she wrote a tarot advice column for the national magazine *Women-in-Touch*.

THE
Language
OF
TAROT

a PROVEN SYSTEM *for* READING *the* CARDS

JEANNIE REED

Llewellyn Publications
Woodbury, Minnesota

FIRST EDITION
First Printing, 2019

Cover design by Kevin R. Brown
Cover illustration 2018 © Chris Lyons / lindgrensmith.com
Interior spreads by Llewellyn Art Department

Llewellyn Publications is a registered trademark of Llewellyn Worldwide Ltd.

Library of Congress Cataloging-in-Publication Data

Names: Reed, Jeannie, author.
Title: The language of Tarot : a proven system for reading the cards / Jeannie Reed.
Description: First Edition. | Woodbury : Llewellyn Worldwide. Ltd, 2019. | Summary: "Learn how to give amazingly accurate, specific, and insightful tarot readings with little or no guesswork. This revolutionary guide, written by a tarot master with 32 years of professional reading experience, reveals a simple, proven system that makes reading cards in a spread nearly as straightforward as reading words on a page"— Provided by publisher.
Identifiers: LCCN 2019023282 (print) | LCCN 2019023283 (ebook) | ISBN 9780738759425 (paperback) | ISBN 9780738759890 (ebook)
Subjects: LCSH: Tarot.
Classification: LCC BF1879.T2 R437 2019 (print) | LCC BF1879.T2 (ebook) | DDC 133.3/2424—dc23
LC record available at https://lccn.loc.gov/2019023282
LC ebook record available at https://lccn.loc.gov/2019023283

Llewellyn Worldwide Ltd. does not participate in, endorse, or have any authority or responsibility concerning private business transactions between our authors and the public.

All mail addressed to the author is forwarded but the publisher cannot, unless specifically instructed by the author, give out an address or phone number.

Any internet references contained in this work are current at publication time, but the publisher cannot guarantee that a specific location will continue to be maintained. Please refer to the publisher's website for links to authors' websites and other sources.

Llewellyn Publications
A Division of Llewellyn Worldwide Ltd.
2143 Wooddale Drive
Woodbury, MN 55125-2989
www.llewellyn.com

Printed in the United States of America

This book is dedicated to Sherri Greene,
student and friend, a gentle soul gone home too soon

Acknowledgments

I want to acknowledge here my amazing agent, Annie Wilder, who was able to see that what I do with tarot is revolutionary and unique and who decided that my work should become this book. Thank you, Annie, from the bottom of my heart.

And I would be remiss if I didn't applaud the downright courage of Llewellyn, my publisher, and Barbara Moore, acquisitions editor, for finding and bringing this work to you.

Finally, thank you, Andrea Neff, Llewellyn production editor, for your scrupulous editorial eye. I am grateful.

DISCLAIMERS

When It Comes to Health and Healing

This book is not intended to provide medical advice or to take the place of medical advice and treatment from your or a client's personal physician. Readers must advise clients to consult their physicians when it comes to medical problems. It is illegal to practice medicine in the United States without a license. If the client suggests otherwise, the reader must be certain to tell the client: (1) "I'm not a doctor" and (2) "I'm not a substitute for a licensed medical doctor. Any information I give you here isn't prescriptive. It's meant to inform. It is not advice."

When It Comes to Legal Issues

The contents of this book are not meant to replace legal protection or help from law enforcement. Readers are advised to contact the proper authorities if they experience harassment, extortion, mental health issues due to threats and fear, actual abuse, or immediate danger. If you work from home or in an isolated setting and you advertise, please try to be certain just whom you're letting into your space. This is particularly true for prospective male clients: listen carefully when they call to make an appointment. You're listening for something "off." Not easy to spot, but please don't assume that everybody out there is "nice." (For safety's sake, this author has always worked only through referral and/or in populated spaces.)

Contents

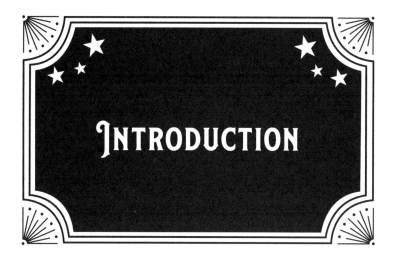

INTRODUCTION

Imagine this:

You're doing a reading and you're looking at the Two of Pentacles reversed (upside down = confusion), and sitting next to it is the Devil (malignancy). Well, you don't have to guess; you *know* that some kind of really serious thing is going on in somebody's mind. Maybe they have dementia. Maybe the person has Alzheimer's disease. Maybe the thinking is "off" because the person had a stroke (if the Tower shows up too). See, you don't have to guess; you just *know*. At the very least, you can whittle down a universe of possibilities to a serious few.

Or say you're looking at a relationship and you see the Two of Cups reversed (no love exchanged or shared) next to the King of Rods / Wands reversed (a man who doesn't want to make a commitment). You don't have to guess; you *know*: a guy who doesn't want to make a commitment is involved in a relationship where there's no love. You can also assume, at least at the start, that these are the cards of the woman.

Or say you're looking at finances and you see the Nine of Pentacles reversed (a joint venture or shared assets—maybe two people own a car together, or a bank account, or land), and next to the nine you see the Seven of Swords (a thief). You don't have to guess; you *know*: there is deception and dishonesty involved in a joint financial arrangement. You tell your client, "Don't get involved." You warn an involved client that their asset is at risk. You wonder out loud, carefully, if your client has something to feel guilty about.

Or say you're looking at a career matter and you see the Four of Cups (an offer; maybe a temptation) and next to it the Ten of Pentacles reversed (insecurity). You don't have to guess; you *know*: the offer will not lead to financial security, and unless the client doesn't care about that, rejecting the offer might be a consideration for the client, no matter how desperate the job seeker is.

This is what I do. This is, in very simple examples, how I do it. This is what you can do too.

But in 1983, when for intensely personal reasons I plunged whole hog into the world of oracles, this stuff was nowhere near the mainstream category of interest it is today. In the "straight" world I was ridiculed. A guy I was seeing told me I was messing with the devil, and it was nearly impossible to find good books and information about any oracle, never mind tarot. (Remember, this was almost twenty years before the internet and Google and the rise of mysticism to a household word.) So when I stumbled on the Samuel Weiser store in Manhattan one day, I felt like I'd died and gone to heaven. There were all kinds of tarot packs, the astrological ephemeris, and books on all kinds of oracular devices. That place was like a knowledge oasis in a desert of mystical ignorance. And for a time it was the only go-to place in all of New York City for an aspiring psychic.

Not that I had any idea at the time that psychic work was to be my future. All I knew was that I needed to be able to access information that was not accessible any other way. I needed to know things hidden in the medically confused mind of the person I loved. And so you can imagine I pursued with a passion all attempts to understand and use *all* the oracles (silly me) available to me at the time, including the *I Ching*, runes, astrology, numerology, and pendulum. Surely one would tell me the answer just like that.

Not.

To be clear: oracles are methods and devices for knowing what's hidden. Knowing the future. Knowing secret thoughts. But not all oracles are the same. Astrology is quite math- and science-based. The *I Ching* is a major literary work. Rune stones, like the *I Ching*, depend on books that translate for the reader the meanings of the symbols on the stones. Palmistry depends on an understanding of the human body and its physical manifestations over time. The pendulum seems to rely on principles of classical physics, and (like all solid oracles) the pendulum can work in the right hands. I've used one a time or two myself, but never with clients. When I work with clients, I need specifics. *They* need specifics. (At a more advanced level are mediumship and automatic writing. I'd love to be able to do this stuff. Maybe one day!)

But unlike all of these other devices and systems, tarot is image-based and the pictures are meant to trigger intuition and right-brain activity. (The right brain is the seat of art, and I've come to believe it is also the sender and receiver of psychic information.) And to this image thing I seemed to respond from day one.

I also have to say that along the way I've discovered we don't necessarily need a well-known oracle to access information hidden from the conscious mind (arcane information). I've done this with the Bible, with Rainer Maria Rilke's *Duino Elegies* poem collection, and even with seemingly random scratchings on the sidewalk, not to mention the pictures in beer foam on the side of a glass.

See, *nothing* is by chance. If you're meant to recognize something that's there right in front of you, you will. What you have to do to get there is to develop your right brain as if it were a muscle. I figured this out twenty years ago. I've read since then that others say the same thing about the brain. (Even IQ isn't static, they've found. Your IQ can go up if you use your mind a lot. I am totally sure my own IQ went up sixteen points just by trying to understand the *I Ching* a few hours every day for months.)

So basically what I'm saying is that the answers are all around us if we know *how* to look and see and how to recognize what we're seeing when we see it.

Which leads me now to explain something: Not everybody is meant to read tarot cards; not everybody is meant to be an astrologer; not everybody is meant to comprehend the *I Ching*; not everybody is meant to solve crimes; not everybody is meant to diagnose illness; not everybody is meant to dispense information on business and finance; not everybody is equipped to understand psychology or physics or biology.

What I'm saying here is that we are all born with certain gifts and potential capabilities. Not all doctors are neurologists or cardiologists or dermatologists, right? While they all practice medicine, each has found his or her own way to the specialty that is the most fulfilling.

And so it was for me and the various oracles. After many, many months attempting to learn the science of astrology, I finally realized that while I can "get" the concepts and certain non-math things, the math and the science of it just isn't for me. Likewise, while I can use the *I Ching* for myself sometimes with great accuracy, it's just too complicated and iffy to try and use with clients. (I've had to face the fact that I'm no master of this absolutely brilliant oracle, despite decades of study and work with it.) And I don't have the slightest interest in knowing how to read a palm.

So, long story short, when I first saw the images that comprise the tarot pack, I was hooked. *This* would work for me! I respond to art, I respond to color, I respond to line and form and the beauty I can see. I once started crying as I walked through a Georgia O'Keeffe exhibit at the Whitney Museum in New York. Something in the pictures just got to me at a very basic emotional level and I suddenly noticed tears were flowing. It was strange. But that is the power of great art and a great artist.

The same thing happens with me sometimes with tarot. Twice, in fact, I found myself crying during a reading. It wasn't because I was sad or the client was in trouble. I was crying because the pictures were so good and so joyful, I was that glad for the client who was getting such beautiful cards.

Another thing: Some people assume my philosophy and beliefs preceded my work with tarot. Not so! Tarot cards, and life, have been *teaching me* most of what I know for over three decades now.

Knowledge Sources

Some people have remarked that the few books I recommend to my students are old. Well, the Bible and the Quran are old too, as is Leonardo da Vinci's Codex. Does it mean they're out of date or invalid or useless? Not in the least. In fact, it means exactly the opposite. If I recommend a book, it's because that book and its thinking have stood the test of time. It's also because the books I recommend to my students formed the foundation of my own work with tarot, including Eden Gray's basic book, *The Complete Guide to the Tarot*; Rachel Pollack's two books on the two Arcana, *Seventy-Eight Degrees of Wisdom* (parts 1 and 2); and Sallie Nichols's *Jung and Tarot: An Archetypal Journey*. These are not "old." In my opinion, they're seminal to my chosen field. In the same way, I recommend without hesitation medium Jeffrey Wands's *Another Door Opens*. This book and its principles will stand the test of time.

As for what is newer and on the shelves now, I have a student who holds a master's degree in finance from Harvard and is studying for a PhD at Columbia University. He also happens to have a *major* gift for psychic work with tarot. He tells me he spent months trying to find a book that would help him learn *practical* tarot, something he could study as if it were a college course and *apply* with total certainty. He tells me he has found it in this book of mine.

Well, that's great, because I wrote this book for exactly that practical purpose, having devoted four years to my own study of tarot as if it were a college course and fifteen years to actual practice before setting pen to paper. This student also tells me that my principles and method work for him, my philosophy is in line with his, and my belief system, rooted as it is in practical things, works for him.

And so I'll continue to recommend the "old" books. See, I stand on the shoulders of those authors. These books are absolutely great. They're thought-provoking and they were written by knowledgeable people with solid and well-developed philosophies.

That's not to say there's nothing else useful out there today. You can go right now to a bookstore or online and find other books that will work for you, and maybe even better than the ones I like to recommend. You may find elsewhere what you personally need to trigger your own responses—the books that work for you and fit your own special talents. See, that's the point: not to consciously read cards but to understand them at some real basic level *without thinking*. It's hard to explain, but you'll know when you get there, in the same way you find yourself driving a car one day without having to think about the mechanics of the car or the rules of the road. You have absorbed the information, and now it's just part of your operating system.

And one more thing about natural ability: I have another student who's been determined for years to use tarot for crime solving, but it's not working for her. See, investigation just isn't in her DNA. This woman, by the way, is becoming a fine medium after years of study and work at it. By the time she's done, she may not even need cards to solve crimes! Her spirit world may inform her, simple as that. In the meantime, though, there are techniques for using tarot to do investigative work. But you have to have it in you to start with. (I spent four years as a private investigator and another three as an investigative journalist, so I guess I *do* have the instinct that's needed for crime-solving work. I'll talk more about this later.)

So how effective is my teaching and my method? Well, a couple of years ago I had a rather large class (seventeen students from all walks of life) for five weeks. During the last session I asked the students to team up, choose somebody famous, and do a reading on that person.

Within minutes, one student pair came up with the fact that Oprah Winfrey would change careers and leave her TV show—and they did this *forty-eight hours before* she made that very announcement. My students put down a row of cards, read them as a string of words, made a sentence, and found Oprah's new life there, as clear as day.

There's a caveat here: As long as you're a student, I think that living public figures are fair game for learning to read cards. But as soon as you're good enough to be in control of the cards every time, you have to stop experimenting with famous living people. We're all entitled to our privacy, right? As learners, though, I know that if we use famous people to practice reading on, we can compare the cards we get and the information we get with the facts we already know about those people's lives. And so we can know which cards we get refer to which parts of life. So far, this is the only way I've found to be certain that students are in fact learning.

In class, this method even works: I think of a person, I draw cards, and a student reads. The students have no idea who I'm thinking of. Doesn't seem to matter! They usually get a lot of accuracy about people I haven't even named.

Progress

It's hard to boil down my own journey from the first pack of tarot to today, but I need to try so you can understand how I got here. Because if you decide to be as dedicated to this as I was, you'll probably have to undertake a similar journey yourself. In the world of tarot, this is the journey of the Fool. It's a wonderful, rich, and brand-new chapter in life.

First, using Eden Gray's *The Complete Guide to the Tarot*, I memorized all the known meanings of the cards (upright *and* reversed). This took maybe a year. Then I started reading for people *without charge*. I was learning and they were my guinea pigs, so how could I charge them? This development of a clientele, during which I often read with a book open in front of me, took another three years.

Finally, late in the fourth year, one of my clients announced that she could no longer "justify taking advantage" of me for free. At the time, I had no idea of the value of my work, so I was surprised. I asked her what I should charge, and she told me. I went along with her recommendation. See, her point was that she was getting such good stuff from me that it was wrong not to compensate me for my efforts. So Melanie Smithson, former accountant and one of my very first clients, launched me on my professional way. Thanks, Mel.

(And here I have to tell you, it's my belief that one of my spirit guides was preparing me and teaching me and finally inspired me when I was ready.)

Actually, that moment was so simple, it's amazing. One day I started thinking about how a rebus works. A rebus is a combination of pictures that translate into words and syllables. For example, I draw an eye (this equals "I"); I insert an addition sign and then draw a heart (this equals "love"); I insert an addition sign and then draw a sheep (this equals "you/ewe"). With the three pictures added together, the rebus says "I love you." All of you are probably already familiar with this. I suppose it's how pre-language people communicated in the first place, with drawings on the walls of caves and drawings scratched in the dirt.

But that aha moment didn't come until about ten years after I'd been reading cards professionally, when I started to realize that tarot cards can be combined (as if with plus signs) and then accurately "translated." There one can find specifics, ideas and information, and all in living color.

At this point I started to think that maybe I could create a system that could be taught and learned—*tarot as science*. I figured that in the same way we learn foreign languages, maybe we could learn to translate cards into words and string them together to equal specific thoughts and ideas—*tarot as a language*. First, I noticed that if the same two cards together *always* indicate abortion for me, for example, then maybe this could be taught and this could be learned. Then I realized that by lining up *more* than two cards in a row across the table, I could read them the way one reads words lined up across a page. A row of cards is a sentence! A row is complete when a thought is complete. I'd never run across another reader who did this, who thought like this, who taught this.

And so I figured if I could be accurate almost every time, then it wasn't guessing anymore. It was more like fact. And facts are what we teach and study and learn in school.

So, bottom line, what I've discovered is that it isn't necessary to put a single card on the table and then try to guess what it might mean. With my method, you can almost always *know* what it means. Imagine how great this is for clients. I never have to say "it feels like" or "it seems like." I can simply say "it *is*." Period. And most of the time they agree with my conclusions.

When I started with tarot, I didn't use the seven-card spread that I use now. The books were full of the Celtic Cross, but this is a very complicated spread (using ten cards to start with) and it's just not suited to answering a single question. (I talk about this spread later in the book.)

A few years after I got into my study though, I "happened" to see a guy named Jeff Norman on local cable TV using seven cards in a certain formation as he read for people who were calling in. (He couldn't see the people. They weren't touching the cards. They were probably miles away. But they were telling him he was being accurate.)

So I decided to adopt the seven-card spread that I continue to use to this day because, basically, it works for me.

After watching Jeff, I also started to question some of the things they say about tarot cards. These days I call them "myths." Feel free to wrap your cards in silk when they're not in use as a sign of respect, as some books recommend, but know that it isn't necessary. The cards themselves have no magical or faith-based properties. I mean, the cards aren't the key to a successful reading. *You* are. (Matter of fact, a lot of times I travel with my cards in a Ziploc bag.)

Which leads me here to tell you that anything you find in this book is not my opinion; it is my *experience*. And there's a big difference. There's also nothing "true" or "false" about what I have to say here. If I learn something from more than one client, it starts to be fact to me. Sure, other books may contradict what I have to say here. That's fine! But if somebody remarks that some of my statements are "untrue," that can't be right, because everything I'm telling you here is the outgrowth of my own personal and professional experience.

As an example, if I know my readings can be accurate for people five thousand miles away whom I cannot see, whom I've never met, and who cannot interact physically with the cards, then I have to figure that *my* clients, at least, don't need to actually touch the cards to get accurate readings, right? And since some of my students are having the same experience, this thing can't just be about physical touch. Instead, it has to be about the reader connecting with the client on some kind of deep level that the tarot images are able to trigger.

I know there are those out there who believe there is a connection that is in fact physical, that physical energy is transferred from one to another through the cards. I respect this. Basically, I respect anything that works! So if this philosophy works for those readers, I can't argue with it. I just know from my own experience that when I work, touch isn't necessary. I know that our connection is huge and invisible and intangible.

Which leads me to another subject: Which tarot pack should you use? Well, not everybody responds to tarot images in the same way, and not all cards are equal. I know which pack is the only one I'll use, while you may respond incredibly well *sub*consciously to an entirely different pack. How can you know it's the right one for you? If people tell you that you're getting accurate and detailed information about them and their lives, then you know you're using the right pack.

I need to say one more thing here, as kind of a warning: Tarot packs that are all pictures of shoes or other objects are not tarot packs. What you want and need is probably either the Rider-Waite pack (which I started with) or a more recent pack based on their designs. See, the Rider-Waite tarot images were very carefully thought out over a hundred years ago, and this pack has inspired hundreds of other packs, including the Morgan-Greer, Robin Wood, Hanson-Roberts, and Aquarian, all of which are in use to this day. This tells us that the Rider-Waite images and thinking have stood the test of time *because they work.*

And this is even more important: Regardless of what tarot pack you use, when your own psychic ability kicks in—and for me this was maybe six years after I started reading professionally—you may start to see things in the pictures that aren't even there but turn out to be true in the client's life. You may even start to see specific images in the worn spots on your cards—and they turn out to be totally accurate too.

See, tarot is designed to trigger *psychic* responses in the reader. First you learn all kinds of things using the left brain (which you use to do math), but then at some point your own gift takes over and bingo, you're saying things you had no idea were even going to come out of your mouth. This stuff just sort of "occurs" to you out of nowhere, and *that* is psychic ability in action. First you learn the mechanics of driving, and then one day you realize you've been doing it for an hour and thinking about everything *but* driving.

The World around Us

You need to know this because maybe you can relate: I was raised a strict, observant Catholic. The work I've been doing for thirty years was described as "devil's work" when I was a kid. Plus, I'm a scientist at heart, meaning I'm a true skeptic. If you can't prove it, I won't believe it. Sorry.

So when I started with oracles, I wasn't ready to believe in anything I couldn't see or touch or explain logically. But then I started to see that oracles work. I could see that divination in the right hands is not fantasy, it is fact. I could see that "reading minds" is totally possible. And so I finally came to understand that what my organized religion had told me was totally not true, at least for me. So I dispensed with the religion, but I kept the faith.

And because at heart I'm still a logical person, once I thought I might have some kind of talent, I had to wonder just *how* I could do what I do. I mean, what is psychic ability? I'd had enough experience by that time to understand that it's no accidental kind of thing that lives somewhere out there in the mists. I recognized that psychic ability must be some kind of serious biological thing. So I started looking for information to explain what I only suspected at that point.

In quantum physics today, there are principles. String theory says that everything and everybody in the universe is connected—we just can't see the connections; we can't see the "strings." Then there was a man named Werner Heisenberg who, in the late 1920s, discovered that we can't ever really know where things are but only where they've been. He told the great Albert Einstein that the very act of observing something changes it. (Imagine how this would work between a psychic and a client. It means there's a constant exchange going on between the two people, who are somehow *already* connected.)

And then there has been research on "photon twinning." Photons are electrical particles in atoms. It has been discovered that if you split a photon in two and shoot the two parts far away from each other and you "injure" one part, the *other* part reacts in real time. Distance does not separate them. (Does distance separate a mother whose son is killed in battle and she knows it *as it is happening*? We all accept that the mother-child psychic bond is primeval and real. And subatomic particles have something just like it? Well, this just amazes me.)

So after a while of seeing TV reports and reading things like that in the paper, I realized it would actually be a miracle if psychic work *didn't* exist.

Bottom line, I have no doubt that I'm connected somehow to my client even before the person gets to my table. Imagine that.

And so over the years I've been able to prove to myself (maybe not to you, but that's your choice) that what I do works and *how* I think it works.

Oops. But is this "spiritual"? No, it isn't. It's pure physics. It's pure biology. Sure, at the beginning of time a great spirit set all of this up. But you can't say arithmetic is "spiritual," right?

So let me say this: My idea of what is "spiritual" has everything to do with faith and my concept of God. But when it comes to psychic work, I never use that word. And there's a really good reason why.

See, I live in Midtown Manhattan, where there are "spiritual advisers" on every corner. These people are nothing but crooks, despite what their signs say. Some have statues of the Holy Family in the window. It makes me nuts. There's even a retired NYPD detective named Bob Nygaard who's made it his life's work to bust as many of these people as he can. They're dangerous to your wallet, they're dangerous to your psyche, and they're dangerous to your emotions. (I should know. I've ended up picking up the pieces of the utter emotional devastation that some of these folks have wreaked on the terrified, dependent, distressed people who trusted them. These "advisers" live in a dark place, and they're skilled at only one thing: separating gullible people from their money. And they call themselves "spiritual.")

So as long as that word is in common usage in that dark place, I will not use it to describe what I do.

Apart from this, I'm convinced that what I do absolutely has to be based in some kind of science. It's just that we don't yet understand it. But as scientists today keep discovering new things about the world around us, maybe in my lifetime something more will surface about psychic work and how it happens. Expect it to come from the modern college physics departments and the Fools there who aren't afraid to explore what they can't even see yet.

So What Can You Expect to Learn Here?

After a while, after keeping track of card combinations that always have the same meaning, I started to think that if I could teach what I do to other people in a classroom-type setting, then maybe I could create a textbook that would do this too.

Naturally, I looked everywhere first for what this book teaches and how it teaches, but as my student had discovered, I couldn't find a thing. So I was kind of pushed into creating my own book, which my students have been using successfully. Along the way, this book has been rewritten three times, as I learned more and came to understand more and wanted people to be able to learn all of that.

And this is important: In every instance—including matters of love, money, career, and finances—what I'm doing is giving the client information they can use *along with what they already know*, so the client can make a good decision. I do not advise. I do not recommend. I'm not the be-all and end-all. I'm not the answer person. I'm just a bridge between the client and what has yet to show up in the client's own conscious mind. Really, I'm like a keyboard to a database. That's all.

Sometimes I even say to clients, "I hope I'm wrong," because sometimes I really am wrong and sometimes what I have to say to them is really unpleasant. Face it. None of us is a god. I keep that in mind 24/7. And before my clients arrive, I say a quick prayer that I'll be able to help them.

As for being wrong, there is one specific instance I need to talk about. It's one thing to have compassion and caring for others, but it's quite another to have heartfelt feelings for those we love. So when I tell you that I've spent thirty-six years studying and working as a psychic and there's not one single thing I can do for myself or for my niece or my sister or anybody else I care deeply about, it's because I care too much that they get only good news. But life isn't like that, right? So I have to send my loved ones to others whose work I respect and who will be able to see them clearly, without bias. In the final analysis, the only thing I can do after all of this studying and effort and experience is to put it at the service of other people. This has been the experience of my students as well.

I can be specific here: Many years ago I was in a devastating emotional state. My marriage was falling apart, which was a very big deal at the time for a good Catholic girl like me. I was aware of the *I Ching* then, so I spent desperate hours one day using it, asking the same question over and over and getting all kinds of stuff that was never the same thing. And suddenly (thank God), I realized I was making myself literally crazy. So I put the book down in fear and I didn't go near it for the next ten years. See, I just wasn't in the right place to be trying to use the occult to solve my problems. (After that, I left the counseling to the professionals trained to do it.) But now I also realize that most of us just care too much about our own outcomes to be able to be dispassionate and objective and therefore correct, at least most of the time, especially with oracular devices that are open to interpretation.

Accept this and you can't go wrong.

And one more thing I have to say here: While the cards that you and your client choose *seem* to be chosen at random from a pile on the table, there is absolutely nothing random going on. The exact right card will be chosen *every time*, face down, even from a pile of seventy-eight cards. This, to my mind, is the *only* thing one needs to take on faith when it comes to reading. I can't *prove* why it's so, so I can't call this part science. The cards that are chosen will combine to tell the right story. Every time.

In fact, I've discovered that even if a card falls out or even flies out of the pack as I'm mixing the cards, it will be the single most important card of the entire reading. Every time.

Here's a good example. I was reading for a married woman who wanted to discuss only her career, when in fact her marriage was in trouble. After about forty-five minutes, the Emperor (husband card) literally flew out of my hands and onto the floor from somewhere in the middle of the pack.

I said, "Well, *he* doesn't want to be ignored!"

So remember,
NOTHING IS RANDOM and EVERYTHING IS PURPOSEFUL,
in life and in readings.

CHAPTER 1
Tarot: Theory and Practice

In this chapter I talk about my philosophy and how I've arrived at the conclusions I've reached about psychic work, psychic ability, and how it all happens. I talk about the subconscious mind and the right hemisphere of the brain and the crucial role I believe they play when psychic talent is engaged and active. I talk about how tarot was designed and what it was designed to do and how that works with us as readers. I talk about having compassion for all people and how that's different from caring for specific people and why this matters.

Over the years I've come to the conclusion that life is a series of cycles, a series of spirals of activity, much like the picture of the DNA helix. These are cycles of accomplishment, growth, and change, each leading to a higher level of ... more cycles. Some philosophers believe that each of us has a predetermined mission. They believe there's an ultimate plateau that each of us must reach in this life, and then life will take on new trappings, through death. I believe this too. In fact, this is the life's work of the great mediums: seeing through that veil of death to what has come before and what is to come. Tarot comprehends the universe, from the smallest living thing to the great and grand schemes of things.

The Arcana

In terms of tarot symbolism, there are two categories of cards. The *Major Arcana* cards represent big life issues, big conditions, long-term things, the macrocosm of life, major dreams, big events, and major decisions. These cards talk about the cycles that spiral upward. In this section of the cards, between the Fool and the World, there is an entire life; and within that life are all the chapters, and each chapter begins with the Fool and ends with the World. So you can see, we just keep cycling upward, and this is called growth. It's amazing that this group of picture cards can be so profound.

The *Minor Arcana* cards, on the other hand, come into play when we talk about the small stuff, the day-to-day stuff. For example, the (Minor) Seven of Swords reversed can mean the client is not being taken advantage of in a particular situation, while the (Major) Justice can mean the client is getting justice on a grand scale, over time. The (Major) Star is about big dreams and long-term aspirations: for example, to be an artist. The (Minor) Seven of Cups is about small dreams, day-to-day things.

It took me a while to realize that there are a lot of parallels between the two groups of cards. It really boils down to the grand scale versus the small scale of things: forest and tree.

Which Tarot Pack Works Best?

I have never met the woman who painted the cards I use, but I am continually astonished at her intuitive ability. It seems she has packed into seventy-eight cards so much *feeling* and so many symbolic things. I've been using this pack for thirty years and I'm *still* finding things I never noticed before. And by the way, as you work with tarot, *it* works at your level of ability. You will get the information you need, when you need it, from whatever pack you use. And when you're ready, you'll get more. It's pretty amazing. The subconscious, I think, guides the learning process, and as we grow more accomplished, we draw more nuanced card combinations because we can handle them.

Another thing about the pack I use is that all the faces of the people in these cards are rich with flesh and emotion. For me this is like gold. As I said, I respond at the emotional level in life and to flesh-and-blood people, so I respond at the emotional level to these cards. I feel things. I can realize the things my client is feeling. I just get it. (The Rider-Waite tarot pack is based in the same symbolism, colors, and images, but the faces are bland. They are not so much human representations as indications. Sure, I can work with these, but the great *psychic* information I get is due, I'm sure, to the very human quality of the "people" in my pack.) Not all of my students agree, but I've noticed that the ones who don't get it have little or no water in their natal astrological chart. They just don't come at life from the heart. They think their way through everything. So maybe they can do serviceable readings, having memorized everything, but maybe they'll never have psychic insight. I'm hoping, though, that as they continue to work with any kind of tarot pack, the power of their right brain will strengthen, slowly but surely.

The Subconscious Mind

What, you may ask, am I talking about here? Good question.

Forty years ago there was a lot of talk that companies were inserting pictures of their products into feature films. So you'd be watching a movie and all of a sudden you'd be craving popcorn. What you didn't know was that you had just *seen* a picture of popcorn, but it went by so fast that your conscious mind didn't know it. Your conscious mind was totally into the movie, so it was your subconscious mind that picked up on it. The seeing of that picture inserted into the film triggered a subliminal response. So you were tricked, really, into craving popcorn. As soon as it was revealed that people were being tricked by things they didn't even realize they were seeing, so-called subliminal advertising was banned, at least so far as they could catch people at it.

Well, I believe that the ideas I get from a group of cards—ideas that seem to have nothing to do with the meanings of these cards—are subliminal responses to what I'm seeing. Maybe it's the combination of colors or the combination of images or some trigger of my own life experience that I don't consciously recognize. See, I don't know for sure. But I do know that I get ideas, that they're accurate, and that they sure aren't necessarily what I'm seeing in the cards in front of me.

And so I have learned that my subconscious must be at work as I read.

I once had an interesting experience with this. The only time I allowed a second person to stay in the room to listen to a reading, totally violating my own rule, I was talking on and on. Suddenly, the client spoke to her friend, who was only about eight feet away on the sofa. My client's voice jolted me out of wherever I was, because I looked up at that friend and what I saw was an incredibly tiny person like a mile away. I was shocked. Where in the world does my head go when I read? Well, wherever it goes, it sure must be the right place.

Again, I need to say that I doubt this will happen for you for a while. As you're starting out, you'll get perfectly accurate and adequate information from the cards you draw, and everything will make sense. And you can do a good job.

But how the subconscious kicks in, and when, is another question. I don't know. It just seemed to start happening to me one day. And that is when I believe my psychic ability kicked in. I said something. Actually, as I said earlier, something just kind of fell out of my mouth, and I was hearing it for the first time myself. I hadn't actually thought it. I just found myself saying it.

Since then, I've "seen" a jigsaw puzzle piece that wasn't there in the throat of the Page of Pentacles, and that child had in fact choked on a jigsaw puzzle piece when he was little. I've seen a 747 in the clouds around the King of Swords, and the person in question was an airline pilot. I've seen a little white dog with black button eyes in the cards of a woman who had such a dog.

Not one of these things is in a tarot pack. Definitely not in mine. But I *saw* them all, as if with my physical eyes. I believe by then I'd worked so hard on my right brain that it was finally just doing its own thing. And, no, I can't explain it.

So, yes, you can just sit down and read cards as an intellectual exercise and be correct. It's what happens with all students of tarot. As I said, I read for people for months with a book open in front of me until I finally learned all the card meanings.

But as time goes on and you work with tarot, you'll start to see more because you'll be developing the right brain (the side that "sees" what isn't there) to the point where it can get information that isn't obvious.

As for tarot cards, as I said, the Rider-Waite pack was carefully thought out and includes colors and forms and symbols designed to trigger not-conscious responses. Take yellow, for example. Real estate agents say, "If you want to sell a house, paint it yellow." Makes sense, right? Yellow is the color of the sun, so it's the color of life. It is a glad color, at least in our culture. So seeing yellow triggers a glad response in us. We don't *think* about it. It's just there. And gray? Well, usually gray is gloomy, right?

In fact, there's a whole body of research on the psychology of color, with conclusions like don't paint prisons red. Keep hospital rooms neutral in color. Wear bright colors to attract. Black, the absence of color, is for mourning the absence of life in our culture.

In addition to color selection, the very designs of traditional tarot cards all call upon archetypes—the moon, the sun, stars, colors, shapes—and we respond to these *without even knowing we're doing it*. An archetype is a sort of icon all humans tend to respond to in the same way. The moon is a romantic thing, for example, to almost everybody. Here again, we're responding in the same way we used to crave that popcorn in the middle of the movie.

Using (Only Half) Your Head

Since I believe that psychic ability is "located" in the right brain, I believe that the potential to use it is there in all of us, to one degree or another. I believe we're born with it. But if all we do is exercise and use the left brain (adding and subtracting our way through school and life), then whatever potential we might have to *be* psychic isn't going to be developed. Don't use a muscle, and it atrophies, right?

The exceptions to this seem to be (a) when we're under extreme emotional duress and (b) when we're sleeping. In both these cases, our defenses are down and glimmers of that native talent can appear. The mother knows when the child is injured. The dreamer has a clear vision of a bad future event. In both these cases, the adding and subtracting side of our head is turned off, which makes room for the creative side to get through to us. This is probably happening all day long, but all day long we're usually focused on work, or at least we're focused on wants, activities, and thoughts. So we don't "hear" what's being told to us by our own "little voices." Believe me, though, they're speaking.

Getting the Messages

So if it's true that we humans can reach out into a kind of ephemeral database and extract information, then when we read cards we're simply using a decoding device to understand *what is inside the people we're reading*. Because we're all connected to the database, right? If I log into Twitter, I'm going to see you and know what you're thinking and doing because you've posted it there. In the same way, our messages are available to others if they know how to look for them.

This is funny. I was once using a very worn pack of cards—half the color was gone—and I started getting accurate information from the worn spots. They *looked* like things to me, in the same way we see faces and shapes in clouds. And because I was focused on the client, the things I was seeing were real—and they were in fact her things.

So how do you know when you're reading well? Simply, you know you're on your way when you can put the book down and get all your information from the cards. As with driving and not paying conscious attention to what you're doing, once you've learned the meanings of the cards and learned the spreads and gotten comfortable with the process of reading other people, reading can become second nature.

To Care or Not to Care

Okay, then. So let's say you've been doing your homework—studying your cards, practicing on people, learning the textbook definitions, and doing exercises to strengthen the creative muscle that is your right brain. And now you think, "Finally, I can read my lover's cards and do a good job." Right? Wrong! Remember, knowing tarot isn't enough.

A successful reading also requires *dis*passion. As a reader, you simply can't care about the *outcome* of a reading. You can care only about doing a good job for the client. If you do start caring about the outcome, your left brain will start calling the shots and you probably won't see what you need to see because you'll be too busy seeing what you *want* to see. See? Any *negative* subliminal message you may get will probably be drowned out by the positive result you want. And so you will learn exactly … nothing at all.

I watched a reader once who was so darn invested in showing off, I was disgusted. She wasn't even good at reading, I knew. But her ego was there, big time, at the total expense of the client. She just didn't care (except, of course, for the fee that was to follow). And this is just bad, bad, bad.

See, what I know is that true reading comes from the heart more than from any other human capacity. It's my compassion that links me to my client. I have to care, not on a personal basis but on a humankind basis. Psychic information comes not from what you think when you look at a card but from what you *feel*. The best stuff is what occurs to you *before* you even have a chance to think. This is why I mentioned earlier that I sit at that table absolutely not judging. We all have faults, flaws, baggage.

And by the way, it doesn't matter if the person you're reading is not a nice person. It *can't* matter if you don't like the person. You still have to care that the person is a human being. Maybe the batterer was battered as a kid. Maybe the jealous person was never cared for, encouraged, supported. It may be hard to arrive at this acceptance and understanding, but it can be done. All it means is that the reader has to be selfless. In the same way a doctor will repair the broken arm of a murderer, we professionals have to work in exactly that way with all who come to us. So I try to stay humble. You need to do that too.

And here is yet another "coincidence."

Not.

An hour after writing the paragraph you just read, I was watching an episode of *Columbo*. And in a gentle way the detective tells the nice old woman he rightfully suspects of murder that "some murderers I even like because they're just nice people." He likes them for who they are; he doesn't like at all what they've done.

So try to be a Columbo when it comes to caring about people in a simply human sense.

CHAPTER 2

The Major Arcana

Before I go further, it's time to give you the card definitions I apply in my own work. In this chapter and the next, you'll find the seventy-eight tarot cards explained as I use them. This is the material you'll have to memorize over time until you have mastery over the cards. Don't rush through this. Read slowly so you can absorb each definition. And do it while you're looking at each card so you start to connect image with meaning. Please note: Not all reverse meanings are the opposite of the upright meanings. Some are just plain different.

A tarot pack contains seventy-eight cards: twenty-two Major Arcana and fifty-six Minor Arcana cards.

The Major Arcana represent the major issues in life, the big things: lifelong dreams, lifelong problems, lifelong situations.

In the story tarot tells, we are born the Fool, naïve and about to start a major journey; and at the end of our lives we experience the World, the end of that journey and the completion of the cycle.

But within this enormous cycle of life are many other cycles, some big, some small. A big cycle might be the length of your marriage(s). A small cycle might be a dinner date with somebody. A big issue might be the fact that you never seem to have justice or fairness in your work life. A small issue might be that your current boss isn't competent, so you're doing all his work as well as your own, for no extra money.

All through our lives, in terms of our cycles, I believe we should be trying to recreate ourselves. I actually love the idea of a new me for a new situation, a new approach, the willingness to learn and adapt to it. On the physical level, in terms of cycles, we know that our bodies are completely new every seven years. During that time, every single cell changes.

Well, this cycling can happen in our daily lives too. And I've come to believe it happens before and after death as well.

So, then, the Major Arcana are the big deals, the macrocosm, the world in which the Minor things take place.

The Major Arcana cards are sometimes hard to put into perspective in a reading because they usually stand for large and imposing issues. But I've also discovered that sometimes a Major card will show up simply because it contains something no other card does. Justice, for example, holds scales, and in many readings for people needing to lose weight, this card shows up. But, of course, it can also be the case that if somebody has been battling weight issues all his or her life, while this card may show up because of the scales, it could *also* mean the reader needs to take into account the face value of the card: it may also mean for this client the truly Major issue of unfairness. Somebody new to tarot doesn't need to know how to see this, but you should know that at some point you will arrive there. Have faith.

Then there are times when one card shows up to stand for two different things, on two different levels.

Again, please don't get too worried about all of this now. For the time being, until you know what you're doing, the cards will simply mean what they mean. No tricky things will be going on. See, I've noticed a wonderful thing. As we progress in our ability to work with tarot, the cards a reader gets become more difficult to understand, but always only to the point where the reader can still do okay.

You will progress at your own pace, and so probably for a long time, Justice will be for you exactly what it is. And this is why you can do accurate, detailed readings with a book open in front of you, looking up every card and working to understand the combinations.

Yes, during this apprentice period it's mostly left-brain work you're doing. But slowly things will start to shift, and your right-brain and purely psychic ability will kick in.

So just work hard and wait for progress to arrive. The looser and more open you are, the less desperate you are to be great or even good, the better you will be as a reader. And remember, keep your ego out of it. You shouldn't feel like bragging when you're correct. You're supposed to be doing a helpful thing for somebody else. That's all. That should be plenty, right? (This is a tough lesson for some of my type-A students who want to master everything yesterday! First I have to teach them to stop that. Then I'm able to teach them tarot.)

Finally, if there are a lot of Major Arcana cards in a spread, you can know that it means there are many huge issues in play at this point in time. The other day I read for somebody and *eighteen* of the twenty-two Major cards showed up almost one after the other. This is an enormous number. Stunning, really. While I wasn't sure exactly how to interpret each of these cards individually, I did know it had to mean huge and significant new things for my client. And by the way, drawing this many Major cards in one spread has happened only one other time in my thirty-five years of reading. Rare, but beautiful to see and feel. And this particular woman is the child of Holocaust victims. I wonder sometimes if there is a connection.

So now here are the definitions of the Major Arcana cards the way I read them. For the purposes of reading tarot the way we read sentences, I give you first a *shorthand* definition and then the more textbook stuff. The shorthand is what I say most of the time when I see each of these cards. It's more like ordinary, everyday language than the way college professors talk.

The Fool

Shorthand: "Look out, world, here I come! I'm ready for anything! I can start brand-new and there's nothing to be afraid of. If I fall, I may bounce, but I won't break."

Traditional: The first principle. Chaos before order is created. Enthusiasm for something new. A sense of adventure. A completely fresh start. Not needing much more than the shirt on your back to leave your comfort zone.

The Fool Reversed

Shorthand: "Suppose I fail? Oh, no, suppose I can't do this? I'm just not ready for a huge leap into a new life. Am I being reckless? Am I being rash?"

Traditional: Not ready to do the next big thing. Afraid to start a big new thing.

The Magician

Shorthand: Having the power to change your life. Having the power to change a situation. Having the power to cure an illness. I imagine a table, I build a table.

Traditional: This card symbolizes the place on the ceiling of the Sistine Chapel where God's finger touches Adam's. It is a doctor, a healer, a bringer of divine energy to Earth. The Magician is a lightning rod that transmits energy from the heavens into the ground. Able to take charge.

The Magician Reversed

Shorthand: No power to change things. No power to change people, though you think or wish you could.

Traditional: No power to heal things. Incurable. Can't make dreams real.

Tip: Many times this card appears in the spread for a wife who thinks she can change her husband, or a woman who thinks she can change a man. But it never happens. It *can't* happen. If somebody doesn't want to change, nothing and nobody is going to "change" that person.

The High Priestess

Shorthand: The ideal. No settling. In a perfect world…

Traditional: There is an arcane tradition that hundreds of years ago there was a female pope. This card symbolizes the veil between what we know and what we cannot know. What is hidden.

The High Priestess Reversed

Shorthand: Settling. Settling for less than you really want. Not ideal.

Traditional: Compromising, but not in a good way. Not demanding the ideal. Maybe potential as an artist or psychic, but no guarantee the gift will be developed.

The Empress

Shorthand: Emotionally ready to be a wife/mother. The *idea* of being a wife/mother.

Traditional: The archetypal wife and/or mother. Able to bear children. Wifehood.

Tip: An archetype is more like the *idea* of what a wife is, for example, than what the actual requirements of being a wife actually are. A woman may think a wife stays home and bakes cookies. That is her idea of wifehood.

The Empress Reversed

Shorthand: Not emotionally ready to be a mother/wife. No longer wanting to be a wife/mother (whether married or not). Divorced. Ignoring the kids emotionally.

Traditional: Not a good mother/wife. Not ready to be a wife/mother.

The Emperor

Shorthand: Emotionally ready to be a husband/father. The idea of being a husband/father.

Traditional: The archetypal husband/father. The chairman of a company. The president of a country. The CEO. A very high-level leader whose title depends on the cards nearby.

Tip: With the Hierophant, this man can be president of a country or head of a church, for example.

The Emperor Reversed

Shorthand: A domineering husband/father, a bully. Not emotionally ready to be a husband/father. Doesn't want to be a husband/father. A lousy husband/father. An incompetent chairman or CEO or president of a country.

Tip: Sometimes a man will appear as the Emperor upside down, yet this same man is pressuring a woman to marry him. Well, you can forget the proposal. He's really not ready. And sometimes a man will think he's a good enough husband or father simply because he conforms to his *idea* of those roles. But who wants to be married to an idea?

The Hierophant

Shorthand: A government. A foreign person. A foreign country. Tradition. A nine-to-five job. Established religion. Bureaucracy. The opposite of art (the High Priestess). Social institutions. The institution of marriage. Government issues (like police, taxes, the court system). Government processes working in your favor.

Traditional: Government, religion, institutions of all kinds, orthodoxy, tradition.

The Hierophant Reversed

Shorthand: Not traditional. Unorthodox. Possibly creative. Bad court decision.

Traditional: Bad government. Cult. Government processes work against you. Creative. Nontraditional. Unorthodox.

Tip: For example, alternative medicine.

The Lovers

Shorthand: Lifestyle change. Time for a lifestyle change. Making a lifestyle change.

Traditional: No difference from my upright meaning.

Tip: This card is particularly misunderstood, as it has nothing now to do with love. Years ago, when a woman married, she left her family home for her husband's home, and this was the choice. Today we interpret the card more generically. The choice for change can be to work a different shift, move to a different kind of place, or use one's leisure time in a different way.

The Lovers Reversed

Shorthand: Needing to make a lifestyle change. Not ready for a lifestyle change. Not ready to make a choice that will decisively alter the rest of one's life.

Tip: Whether this card appears right-side up *or* upside down, it usually means the change is necessary soon.

The Chariot

Shorthand: Having one's act together. A vehicle. Having one's act together and taking it on the road. The emotions and the intellect working in perfect harmony. Short trips.

Traditional: The triumph of the superego over the id and ego. Someone coming who has his or her act together.

The Chariot Reversed

Shorthand: Not having one's act together A bad or unreliable vehicle. Stalls. No movement. Either the intellect or the emotions are too prominent. Imbalance.

Tip: Danger driving a car, especially with the Five of Swords reversed (anger: road rage) and/or the Knight of Swords reversed (destructiveness).

Strength

Shorthand: "I believe in me. I have faith in me. I believe in God. I have faith in God." Health. The ability to control one's desires and urges. Physical strength. Self-love. Self-esteem. Healthy immune system. The ability to be tolerant.

Tip: The symbol is a woman holding firm the jaws of the lion. The image on this card in the Rider-Waite deck tells us we are both human *and* beast, and our higher self must always be in charge. But sometimes we are too tolerant about things that should simply be abandoned, because what we are really doing is settling and probably not wanting to admit it.

Strength Reversed

Shorthand: No faith in self. No faith in God. Infection. Despair. Compromised immune system. An appetite out of control. Excess. Susceptibility to disease.

The Hermit

Shorthand: Shedding light on something. Wisdom. A wise person. A person trained to illuminate the dark places. Aloneness. Looking within. Solitude. Wise person. Giving counsel or enlightening.

Tip: For me, this card with the Moon is psychotherapy.

The Hermit Reversed

Shorthand: Refusal to listen to good advice.

Traditional: Not alone. Not wise. Not in a position to give counsel or shed light. Immaturity.

The Wheel of Fortune

Shorthand: It's time. The tide is in and it's time to launch something.

Traditional: Optimism. Growth. Fortune (good or bad). A cycle: maybe a day, a week, a month, a year, a decade, etc. Motion.

Tip: When this card appears, it usually means it's time to take a big step.

The Wheel of Fortune Reversed

Shorthand: It's not time. The tide is out.

Traditional: Nothing coming fast or soon. Stalled. Slump. Stoppage.

Tip: This card usually means it's not time to do something big.

Justice

Shorthand: Getting what you deserve or have earned (in a good way). A legal decision. A legal document. The law. Balance. Weight issues (whether the issue is out of control or not depends on nearby cards). Being deserving. Fairness.

Tip: When this card appears only to convey the idea of scales, whether it's about weight that is out of control or not depends on nearby cards. With Temperance reversed, for example, I read it as weight out of control (obesity, anorexia, etc.).

Justice Reversed

Shorthand: Not getting what you deserve or have earned. Injustice. Problems with the law or legal issues. Unfairness. Out of balance. Not being treated fairly. Bad law.

Tip: With the Seven of Swords, this card can be talking about crime.

The Hanged Man

Shorthand: Hanging around. Patience. Something pending. Philosophical while waiting.

Traditional: Willingness to surrender physical needs to spiritual development (for example, as in Alcoholics Anonymous, Narcotics Anonymous, Gamblers Anonymous, and so forth). Able to make sacrifices. Holy. The need to favor a leg or foot, usually because of injury. The ability to compromise.

Tip: Patience is not always a good thing if you're being patient with a bad person or situation.

The Hanged Man Reversed

Shorthand: "When is it *my* turn?"*

Traditional: Impatience. Not willing to wait and be philosophical and accepting about something.

Tip: *In my system, this attitude is never selfish; it's healthy if you've been choosing to play second fiddle to somebody or something for too long.

Death

Shorthand: Maturity. Maturing. Slow growth.

Traditional: Rebirth. See the sun rising? A cycle is beginning. Shedding a skin, like a caterpillar transforming into a butterfly. The Saturn cycle in astrology. Leaving behind the conditioning of the family to become your own person. Developing your own ideas and opinions (usually happening between the ages of twenty-eight and thirty-one).

Death Reversed

Shorthand: Immaturity. Grow up, already! Still in bondage to early family conditioning and/or lessons.

Temperance

Shorthand: Holistic health. Balance. Eating right. Drinking in moderation. Hormonal balance. Water intake. Friendship. Healthy routines. Desire to heal and/or nurture others. Cooking. Sometimes bartending.

Traditional: Holistic health. Balance. Moderation. Groups and/or organizations. Philanthropy.

Temperance Reversed

Shorthand: An out-of-control bad habit. Too much salt and/or sugar in the diet. Too little water in the diet. Not holistically healthy.

Traditional: Intemperate. Need for exercise and/or dieting.

Tip: This card with the Devil can mean addiction, obesity, or alcoholism. (Remember learning about the temperance movement, when ladies went around the United States smashing the liquor bottles from saloons?)

The Devil

Shorthand: Malignant. Chronic. Toxic. Very bad. Crutch issues. Sick. Great sex.

Traditional: Bad. Illness. Evil.

Tip: With certain other cards, the Devil can mean addiction, compulsion, or obsession. This card mostly influences anything around it in a really bad way. We all have devils within us, the seeds of bad things we're usually able to stop ourselves from doing.

The Devil Reversed

Shorthand: Not bad, toxic, or malignant. Healed. Letting go of unhealthy crutches.

Traditional: You may notice in the image on this card in the Rider-Waite deck that the chains linking the people to the Devil are loose around their necks. All they have to do is lower their heads and the chains will fall off. And so, we can overcome even our most terrible problems. When this card is reversed, the chains automatically fall off.

The Tower

Shorthand: Shake up your life. Your life is being shaken up. Radical change. Electric and electronic things.

Traditional: Revolution. The unexpected. Explosion. (The theory here is that change equals growth.)

Tip: This card can also show up to reflect a stroke or a neurological problem in the upper body. Something drastically changes your life or a major aspect of it. If it's a job, for example, you quit or you're fired. Either way, this card shows up.

The Tower Reversed

Shorthand: Conflict. Inner conflict. Conflict with another.

Tip: This card can also show up to reflect a neurological problem in the lower body or an injured ankle or foot.

The Star

Shorthand: Aspirations. Big dreams. Long-term dreams. Lifelong dreams. Hope.

Traditional: Lodestar. Philanthropy. In sync with the forces of the universe and of nature.

The Star Reversed

Shorthand: Depression.

Traditional: Resignation. Unfulfilled dreams. Nothing to look forward to or hope for.

The Moon

Shorthand: Mother. The womb. The instincts. The public. The animal kingdom. The subconscious. Controlling mother. Dreams while sleeping. Primal mother. Reproductive system. Psychology. Retail sales. One bodily organ (as opposed to the kidneys, for example, of which there are two).

Traditional: A feminine archetype. Nurturing.

Tip: This was the hardest card for me to learn. It seems to go in so many different directions.

The Moon Reversed

Shorthand: Reunion. Going back to someone or something.

The Sun

Shorthand: A new life (at any age). Daytime. The life force. Enthusiasm. A baby. A birth.

The Sun Reversed

Shorthand: The meaning is the same as when the card is right-side up.

Tip: I've never seen this card be negative in any way.

Judgment

Shorthand: Wake-up call. Realizing something (usually a big something). Making a major announcement. Hearing a major announcement.

Traditional: Hearing long-awaited news.

Judgment Reversed

Shorthand: Not realizing. Needing to realize something. Not aware of something. Not yet aware. Needing to be aware.

The World

Shorthand: Successful completion. Closure. End of a cycle. Christmas season.

Traditional: Celebration. The end of the Fool's journey.

Tip: A successful completion can be anything one finishes, even when it's bad. (For example, leaving a bad marriage is a successful act.)

The World Reversed

Shorthand: No successful completion. No closure. Unfinished business that will stay unfinished.

CHAPTER 3

The Minor Arcana

In this chapter you will learn the meanings I use for the fifty-six Minor Arcana cards. In the pack I use, the suit of Wands is called *Rods*. And when it comes to the shorthand and traditional definitions, I have found over the years that if the traditional definitions work just fine with my system, I'm calling them shorthand and leaving it at that. As I said, I stand on the shoulders of masters; there's no need to try and reinvent a perfect wheel. Also, not all of my cards have literally opposite meanings when upright or reversed. Some reverses introduce totally new concepts. The shorthand definitions are the ones I usually apply and are listed in my own order of priority. Finally, as with the Major Arcana, I don't have tips for every Minor card. If you refer to the lists of card combinations that come later in the book, that should be enough to learn from.

To use an analogy, if the Major Arcana can be compared to a big thing, like a year, then the Minor Arcana can be compared to a small thing, like a day.

There are fifty-six Minor Arcana cards. These are comparable to a Texas Hold'em poker deck, with the addition of four Knights. Also, in tarot, we see Pages instead of Jacks in the Court Cards. And as with regular playing cards, the Minor Arcana is divided into four suits: Cups (hearts), Pentacles (diamonds), Rods/Wands (clubs), and Swords (spades).

Because this is so, I was able to read cards using a regular poker deck for a long time, until I lost my fear of tarot and plunged into this beautiful new world. I guess the Fool (me) was ready at last!

Now, when you're doing a reading and many cards of the same suit fall together in a spread, it means there is an emphasis on that category. The categories are as follows:

Cups = Love, fulfillment, satisfaction, dreams, emotions

Pentacles = Money, work, career, physical/material things

Rods/Wands = Energy, dynamism

Swords = Angst, pain, problems, intellect

So, for example, if you lay down seven cards and three or more cards are Pentacles, you can be pretty sure that money and/or work is somehow important in the overall picture. Along the same lines, if you're reading a hardcore businessperson, you might *expect* to see a lot of Pentacles—work is the person's life, after all. But if you don't, it can be equally informative. The CEO of a company with a lot of Cups in a spread will make for an interesting client!

In terms of a well-known example, years ago I heard an interview with Donald Trump and his wife at the time, Marla Maples. Before he became president of the United States, Trump said he loved to "make calls to bankers" in the middle of the night (Pentacles), whereas Marla Maples said she loved to "walk on the beach" (Cups). I wondered at the time about their compatibility.

In certain tarot packs you will find beautiful emotionally reflective faces. Look through these cards and try to *feel* what you're seeing in the faces. This exercise is engaging all of you and not just your head/left brain.

Here are the meanings of the Minor Arcana cards.

• • • CUPS • • •

Ace of Cups

Shorthand: Having love to offer. Able to love. Fulfillment. Gratification. Pleasure.

Traditional: The above, plus: Beginning of a creative exercise. A creative idea. Talent.

Ace of Cups Reversed

Shorthand: No love to offer. Empty inside. Not fulfilled. Not gratified.

Traditional: Lacking talent.

Two of Cups

Shorthand: Two people in love. Love shared. A meeting of the minds and hearts.

Traditional: Sharing. Sympatico. A creative collaboration.

Two of Cups Reversed

Shorthand: Two people not in love. Two people no longer in love.

Three of Cups

Shorthand: Friends. Emotional support from friends. Nurturing friend(s). Social life. Partying. Networking.

Traditional: Social gathering. Good relationships with non-family. Three people. Sometimes a wedding celebration or bridal shower.

Three of Cups Reversed

Shorthand: No friends. No emotional support from friends. Not enough social life. Needing a social life. Needing some fun. Needing to network.

Four of Cups

Shorthand: Being tempted by something or somebody. Considering an offer.

Traditional: Needing to decide or choose. Something on offer.

Tip: The offer or temptation can be about love or a job. Keep adding cards until you know which it is.

Four of Cups Reversed

Shorthand: Accepting an offer. Succumbing to temptation.

Tip: Add cards until you know which of these two options it is.

Five of Cups

Shorthand: Regret. Living in the past.

Traditional: Not seeing the potential for the future. Not yet over a loss.

Tip: The person in the image on this card in the Rider-Waite deck is so focused on the spilled cups that he or she doesn't realize there are two full cups behind him or her. This person would not be ready for marriage, for example, even if it's somebody proposing marriage to another.

Five of Cups Reversed

Shorthand: No longer regretful. No longer living in the past. Ready to look ahead.

Six of Cups

Shorthand: Early childhood. Siblings. People you've known since childhood.

Traditional: Protective and sheltering. Nuclear family. Good childhood. Good conditioning.

Tip: Often this card can refer to a family member, but not the child or the husband or wife of the client.

Six of Cups Reversed

Shorthand: A child not loved by the mother the way he or she needed to be. Not a nurturing, happy childhood.

Traditional: Lack of support from family members during childhood.

Seven of Cups

Shorthand: Day-to-day dreams. Dreaming of…

Traditional: Ideas about things not necessarily emotional in nature. A state of inaction while you're thinking creatively.

Seven of Cups Reversed

Shorthand: Making your dreams come true.

Traditional: Making real what you have imagined, usually on a small scale.

Eight of Cups

Shorthand: In denial.

Traditional: Turning your back on pleasure to look within. Meditation. Higher education. Seeking wisdom. Able to be a "monk" for a while in order to learn things about oneself.

Tip: In the image on this card in the Rider-Waite deck, notice the cups that the person is turning his or her back on for the time being.

Eight of Cups Reversed

Shorthand: "Been there, done that, now I know better." Coming back to life after learning something.

Traditional: Partying. Back and fully engaged in your day-to-day life.

Nine of Cups

Shorthand: Joy. Elation. Fulfillment. Gladness. You get your wish. Your cup runneth over.

Tip: This is traditionally known as the "wish card." If it's the last card in a spread, it's very good.

Nine of Cups Reversed

Shorthand: No joy. Not happy. You don't get your wish.

Ten of Cups

Shorthand: A happy, love-filled marriage.

Ten of Cups Reversed

Shorthand: Not a happy, love-filled marriage. Unhappy marriage. The love in the marriage is gone.

Page of Cups

Shorthand: An adult who has been healed through psychotherapy. A sweet child.

Traditional: A water-sign child (Pisces, Cancer, Scorpio). An artistic child. A dreamer child.

Tip: Look to the other cards in the spread to determine if the child is now an adult. For example, you see as well the Queen of Cups *right-side up* (no settling allowed) or the King of Cups (a loving man) or the High Priestess (no settling/the ideal). If we love ourselves, we won't accept less than what we really want/need, unless we have a very good reason for it.

Page of Cups Reversed

Shorthand: A child or an adult not loved in childhood by the mother the way the child needs or needed to be. The person's emotional needs were not met by the mother. An emotionally wounded child all grown up but not healed.

Tip: I refer such people to psychotherapy to repair the wounds inflicted by the mother's neglect of the child's emotional needs.

Knight of Cups

Shorthand: Contemplation.

Traditional: Romantic. Artistic. A water-sign youth (Cancer, Scorpio, Pisces; maybe eighteen to twenty-three years old). Poet.

Tip: Add cards until you know what exactly is being contemplated.

Knight of Cups Reversed

Shorthand: Seduction or a seducer (never good and not always sexual).*

Traditional: Immature. Lustful.

Tip: *Many not-good things can be seductive, like considering the wrong job for the wrong reasons.

Queen of Cups

Shorthand: A woman who values herself. A woman who doesn't sell herself short. A woman who loves herself and will not settle.

Traditional: An emotional woman. A water-sign woman (Cancer, Scorpio, Pisces). A contemplative woman. An artistic woman.

Queen of Cups Reversed

Shorthand: A woman who sells herself short. A woman who doesn't love herself and is in need of psychotherapy. A woman who settles for men who don't love her. A woman who doesn't get what she needs emotionally.

Tip: In the extreme, this card can be a prostitute.

King of Cups

Shorthand: An emotionally healthy man. A man who knows how to love. A man who can feel love.

Traditional: A creative man. An unselfish man. A water-sign man (Cancer, Scorpio, Pisces). Giving. Sensitive.

King of Cups Reversed

Shorthand: A man who can't love. A man who won't fulfill *any* woman's needs. A selfish man.

Traditional: A selfish man. A noncreative man. A self-indulgent man. A manipulative man. An insensitive man.

Tip: No doubt this man's emotional needs were neglected by his mother when he was little. He needs to go to psychotherapy if he is to be able to enter into a giving, fulfilling, sharing relationship.

• • • PENTACLES • • •

Ace of Pentacles

Shorthand: An opportunity. A breakthrough.

Traditional: The beginnings of money. A seed. A growth (medical). Conception. Food.

Ace of Pentacles Reversed

Shorthand: No opportunity. No breakthrough. Bad knee. Calcification. Gestation period. Need vitamins.

Traditional: Delay. Stoppage.

Two of Pentacles

Shorthand: Handling things. Coping. Dating. Juggling finances. Two sources of income. Two locations. Two jobs. Two-unit body parts (such as the kidneys, eyes, lungs, breasts, ovaries, etc.). Reel-to-reel (in the film world).

Two of Pentacles Reversed

Shorthand: Can't cope. Can't handle something. Can't juggle things successfully. Not dating. Can't pay the bills. In over one's head, usually financially.

Three of Pentacles

Shorthand: A skilled job. A high-level job. The skill to do a high-level job.

Traditional: Skilled tradesperson. Journeyman. Craftsman. Artisan.

Tip: This is a step above the Eight of Pentacles in terms of skill level.

Three of Pentacles Reversed

Shorthand: Not a high-level job. Not a job requiring a high skill level.

Traditional: Not having a great skill set. Not working.

Four of Pentacles

Shorthand: Hanging on for dear life to something we should be letting go of. Clinging.

Traditional: Holding on. Greediness. Crutches.

Four of Pentacles Reversed

Shorthand: Letting go of something that isn't good for us. Getting up out of the chair and walking.

Traditional: Letting go of an emotional or psychological crutch. No longer clinging. Spending money.

Five of Pentacles

Shorthand: Looking for a job or a home.* An orphan in the real sense, though the odd kid in a family can feel like an orphan. Looking for a place to belong.

Traditional: Out of work. Homeless. Out in the cold. Feeling lost. Outside what is socially acceptable, like an adulterer.

Tip: *If you keep adding Cups to the spread, you can assume it's a home; Pentacles means a job.

Five of Pentacles Reversed

Shorthand: Finding a job or a home. Finding a place where you feel you belong. Finding your place in the world.

Six of Pentacles

Shorthand: Positive cash flow. Income.

Traditional: Sharing. Generosity. Spending money. Occasionally, philanthropy. On the giving or receiving end of a gift. Having enough to donate to those less fortunate.

Six of Pentacles Reversed

Shorthand: Negative cash flow. Not making enough money.

Traditional: Not having or earning enough to share.

Seven of Pentacles

Shorthand: What's the point of even bothering? A cost-benefit analysis. Putting a lot into something and not getting a heck of a lot back—is it worth it?

Seven of Pentacles Reversed

Shorthand: Boredom. Tedium. Pushing paper around (like at an office).

Eight of Pentacles

Shorthand: A job with a learning curve. A challenging job that develops existing skills. Enthusiastic about the job. On-the-job training.

Traditional: An apprentice (usually reporting to a Three of Pentacles person). Working on whatever is indicated in the spread: sometimes this can even be a relationship, though this is rare. (In any case, add cards until you're sure what's going on.)

Tip: You will probably see the Page of Pentacles (student) in a spread with this Eight, which means on-the-job training and classroom work: practice and theory.

Eight of Pentacles Reversed

Shorthand: Not a challenging job. A menial job. A low-level job.

Nine of Pentacles

Shorthand: "I have built my world, and even if I am alone in it for now, I love what I have made." An entrepreneur. An independent woman or man. Self-employment.

Tip: This is my favorite card in the pack because it tells me the client is solid, standing up, and fulfilled, even if he or she is alone for the moment.

Nine of Pentacles Reversed

Shorthand: A joint financial venture. Joint finances. Shared money. Shared asset(s). A business partnership.

Tip: There is nothing negative in the Nine of Pentacles reversed unless "bad" cards fall on it or next to it.

Ten of Pentacles

Shorthand: Emotional and/or financial security.

Traditional: Inheritance. Family money. An estate. An empire or a dynasty. A family business. Extended family. Generations.

Ten of Pentacles Reversed

Shorthand: Emotional and/or financial insecurity.

Traditional: Disinheritance.

Page of Pentacles

Shorthand: A student. Training. Studying in a classroom and/or from books.

Traditional: An earth-sign child (Taurus, Virgo, Capricorn). A practical child.

Tip: This card is often found in the same spread with the Eight of Pentacles (on-the-job training).

Page of Pentacles Reversed

Student: Needing to study but resisting it. Needing to go to school. Interrupted education.

Traditional: An impractical child

Tip: I would hope all children are impractical, but that's just me.

Knight of Pentacles

Shorthand: Self-reliance. The ability to stand on one's own two feet without needing emotional or financial help or a crutch. Self-sufficient.

Traditional: An earth-sign youth (Taurus, Virgo, Capricorn). A workhorse. A practical youth.

Knight of Pentacles Reversed

Shorthand: Unable to stand on one's own two feet. Unstable. Not self-sufficient.

Queen of Pentacles

Shorthand: The right job.

Traditional: A woman who can successfully handle both career and family. An earth-sign woman (Taurus, Virgo, Capricorn). A practical woman. A nurturer.

Queen of Pentacles Reversed

Shorthand: The wrong job.

Traditional: A woman who cannot nurture a family and have a career at the same time. There can be problems with the reproductive system. Having trouble conceiving.

King of Pentacles

Shorthand: A man willing to be depended on. A man willing to be relied on. A provider. A breadwinner. A supportive man (can be emotional or financial support or both).

Traditional: An earth-sign man (Taurus, Virgo, Capricorn). Financier. Landlord. A man of property who might be generous with what he has. A successful man by his own standards.

King of Pentacles Reversed

Shorthand: A man not willing to be relied on. A man who doesn't want to be a provider. A man who doesn't want to provide emotional and/or financial support.

Tip: Clearly, this guy is not a good partnership prospect.

• • • Rods/Wands • • •

Ace of Rods/Wands

Shorthand: Pure energy. Starting to put energy into something.

Traditional: Potential for writing and/or acting. Protein. Hair. Penis.

Ace of Rods/Wands Reversed

Shorthand: No energy going into something. Lacking protein. Maybe sperm problems.

Two of Rods/Wands

Shorthand: Thinking (add cards until you know what is being thought about). Not ready to act yet.

Traditional: Something has been accomplished and something else is now in hand.

Two of Rods/Wands Reversed

Shorthand: Confusion. Can't think.

Three of Rods/Wands

Shorthand: Thinking about the next step. A relationship is working.

Traditional: Two things done, another in hand. Looking for growth. Ready to move on. Coastal areas. Distant shores.

Three of Rods/Wands Reversed

Shorthand: A relationship has broken down.

Four of Rods/Wands

Shorthand: A good home or work environment (add cards until you know which it is). Living together (can be roommates).

Four of Rods/Wands Reversed

Shorthand: Not a good home or work environment. Disruption in the home or work environment. Moving. Leaving home.

Five of Rods/Wands

Shorthand: Busy. Lots of activity.

Five of Rods/Wands Reversed

Shorthand: Resolving a problem.

Six of Rods/Wands

Shorthand: Winning. Victory. You get what you want. Moving forward on your own terms. Recognition for an accomplishment.

Traditional: An award. Moving with confidence into the future.

Six of Rods/Wands Reversed

Shorthand: Losing. Not victorious. You don't get what you want.

Traditional: No recognition for efforts.

Seven of Rods/Wands

Shorthand: Sending out résumés, if a worker. Building a clientele, if self-employed. Perseverance leads to success.

Traditional: Having the upper hand. Using all the means at your disposal to get something accomplished.

Seven of Rods/Wands Reversed

Shorthand: Need to send out résumés. Need to build a clientele. Not having the upper hand. Doubts.

Traditional: Time to start looking for something better.

Eight of Rods/Wands

Shorthand: Any minute now. Something's "in the air." Moving rapidly toward something or something moving rapidly toward you.

Traditional: Something's on the way. Air travel. Soon.

Eight of Rods/Wands Reversed

Shorthand: Don't hold your breath waiting. Stuck.

Traditional: Stagnation. Nothing coming soon. No travel. Stalled. Interrupted flight.

Nine of Rods/Wands

Shorthand: Protecting what you have accomplished so far.

Traditional: Resting between battles. Wary. Watchful. Defenses alert.

Nine of Rods/Wands Reversed

Shorthand: "I give up." Throwing in the towel. Not protecting what you have accomplished so far.

Traditional: Defenses down. Defenseless. Lacking vitality / energy.

Ten of Rods/Wands

Shorthand: Eventually. Keep going and for sure you'll eventually get where you're trying to go. Stamina.

Traditional: Strong back. You will eventually reach your desired destination.

Ten of Rods/Wands Reversed

Shorthand: Burnout. Exhaustion. Really needing a vacation or rest. Susceptible to disease. No stamina. Hair loss.

Traditional: Not going to get where you want to go. No energy.

Tip: When I see this card, I warn the client to get plenty of rest and nutrition.

Page of Rods/Wands

Shorthand: Talking about something. Hearing something.

Traditional: A fire-sign child (Aries, Leo, Sagittarius). Announcements. Communication. Speaking. Singing. Acting.

Page of Rods/Wands Reversed

Shorthand: Repression. Not listened to when a child. Burying bad feelings and truths inside. Not telling what needs to be told (for example, in psychotherapy). Not communicating.

Knight of Rods/Wands

Shorthand: Focusing on … (add cards until you know what the focus is).

Knight of Rods/Wands Reversed

Shorthand: Need to focus on … (add cards until you know what the focus needs to be).

Queen of Rods/Wands

Shorthand: A woman willing to commit to being a wife/mother. A wife. A mother. A woman capable of making a commitment. A sister or a woman who is like a sister.

Traditional: A fire-sign woman (Aries, Leo, Sagittarius). An actor. A writer. A good manager. A good communicator. A dynamic woman. A faithful woman.

Queen of Rods/Wands Reversed

Shorthand: A woman who doesn't want to be a wife/mother (she can be married at the time). A woman who was too young when she had her kids to be the mother they needed.

Traditional: Not ready for motherhood. An immature female. An unfaithful female. A woman who doesn't want to make a commitment. A poor manager.

King of Rods/Wands

Shorthand: A man willing to commit to being a husband/father. A good manager/boss. A thoughtful man. A man capable of making a commitment. A brother or a man who is like a brother.

Traditional: A fire-sign man (Aries, Leo, Sagittarius). A fatherly man. A virile man. A dynamic man. A faithful man.

King of Rods/Wands Reversed

Shorthand: A man not willing to make a commitment. A man not loyal. Not good husband/father material. A man not ready for an emotional commitment.

Traditional: An immature man. An uncommunicative man.

Tip: This card is not so good if it's a guy with a spouse and/or kids, or a man unwilling to make a true commitment but getting married anyway. He won't necessarily be faithful.

• • • SWORDS • • •

Ace of Swords

Shorthand: Making a decision. A big decision. Decisiveness. Knife/scalpel. Surgery. Biopsy. Needle. Injection.

Traditional: Keen. Sharp.

Tip: Sometimes a decision is made not to decide, or a decision is made *to* decide.

Ace of Swords Reversed

Shorthand: Not making a decision. Biopsy. Needle. Injection.

Traditional: Not keen. Not sharp.

Two of Swords

Shorthand: Not making a decision with emotional implications.

Two of Swords Reversed

Shorthand: Making a decision even though it has emotional implications. Deciding.

Three of Swords

Shorthand: Pain. The "pits." Hurts a lot. Lousy job.

Traditional: A love affair built on someone else's pain. Broken heart. Medically there can be a cardiovascular problem.

Tip: Rarely for me does this card mean an emotional triangle.

Three of Swords Reversed

Shorthand: Still hurts, but not as much as before. Medically there can be a cardiovascular problem.

Traditional: Time heals.

Four of Swords

Shorthand: On hold (a person, a plan). In the recovery room (figuratively or literally).

Traditional: Needing to recover. Not yet back to life. Inaction.

Tip: The person in the picture is not dead. The hand is very much alive.

Four of Swords Reversed

Shorthand: No longer on hold. Back to life.

Traditional: Ready to try again. Recovered.

Five of Swords

Shorthand: A psychological pattern of failure. Futility. (Something is) in vain. Recidivism. Relapse.

Tip: The image implies the thieves will be back.

Five of Swords Reversed

Shorthand: Anger / frustration. Violence (add cards until you know who or what is under attack). Brutality.

Six of Swords

Shorthand: Taking yourself away from a lousy situation under your own steam. Journey by water.

Tip: We learn from our pain(s). The three people in the boat in the image on the card in the Rider-Waite deck are usually three different aspects of the same person. You don't need to know which aspects. And the knives (the pain) are keeping the boat afloat.

Six of Swords Reversed

Shorthand: Not taking yourself away from a lousy situation.

Traditional: Stagnation.

Seven of Swords

Shorthand: Dishonesty. Deception. Guilt. Betrayal. (The guilt / betrayal can be the client's own.) A thief. Crime. Theft. Politics in the workplace.

Traditional: Disingenuousness. Sneakiness. Politics in the workplace. Gambling (including legal gaming). Bad motive.

Seven of Swords Reversed

Shorthand: Innocent. Pure of heart. Honesty. Straightforward.

Traditional: Not malicious. No bad motive.

Eight of Swords

Shorthand: Hostage to a situation. Hands are tied and can't see what to do. Trapped.

Traditional: Surrounded by difficulty. In exile / away from your society.

Eight of Swords Reversed

Shorthand: Free. Breaking free. Setting yourself free.

Nine of Swords

Shorthand: Grief. A crying child. Devastating emotional pain. Weeping in the middle of the night.

Traditional: Rivers of tears.

Nine of Swords Reversed

Shorthand: Still hurts, but not as bad as before.

Traditional: There's just a dull ache now, emotionally. Life isn't happy, but at least you're not crying all the time anymore.

Ten of Swords

Shorthand: It's always darkest just before the dawn. Things cannot get worse. Down but not out. There's light at the end of the tunnel.

Ten of Swords Reversed

Shorthand: The worst is over.

Page of Swords

Shorthand: Ready to make a decision. Making a decision, though maybe being a bit timid about it.

Traditional: An air-sign child (Gemini, Libra, Aquarius). A thoughtful child. Early intellectual stage.

Tip: The Page's sword is not complete, whereas the Ace's sword is complete. I see this as a timid decision as opposed to a solid, confident decision.

Page of Swords Reversed

Shorthand: Not ready to make a decision, although a decision is called for.

Knight of Swords

Shorthand: Out of the blue. Suddenly. The unexpected.

Traditional: An air-sign youth (Gemini, Libra, Aquarius).

Tip: The thing that suddenly happens can be either good or bad.

Knight of Swords Reversed

Shorthand: Destructive. Self-destructive. Violent. An attack.

Queen of Swords

Shorthand: A smart woman. A sharp woman. A decisive woman. A cold woman. A cold mother.

Traditional: An agent. A lawyer. A doctor. An air-sign woman (Gemini, Libra, Aquarius). An editor. An intellectual female.

Queen of Swords Reversed

Shorthand: A critical mother. An unloving mother. A cold mother.

Traditional: An incompetent lawyer or doctor. An incompetent agent.

King of Swords

Shorthand: A smart man. A sharp man. A decisive man. An agent. A lawyer. A doctor.

Traditional: An air-sign man (Gemini, Libra, Aquarius). An intellectual man. A pilot. Sometimes a dentist. Sometimes a surgeon.

King of Swords Reversed

Shorthand: An indecisive man. Not a loving man. A critical man. A nasty man. An incompetent lawyer. An incompetent agent.

CHAPTER 4

THE PEOPLE CARDS

In this chapter you'll find information about the tarot people and personalities. As in life, these folks are gay and straight, and they have feelings, thoughts, dreams, hopes, fears, anxieties, skills, deficiencies, warts, and flaws. In other words, they're just plain human.

I've discovered some things along the way that I'd like to pass along about the "people" cards. These are formally known as the Court Cards: Pages, Knights, Queens, and Kings.

The Animus and the Anima

Early in the last century, Carl Jung called our other-gender component the *animus* (masculine, for a woman) and the *anima* (feminine, for a man). In the past couple of decades there's been a lot of talk about the male's sensitive, feminine side. Well, that in a nutshell is the *anima*. Women cry, and it's expected. Men cry, and finally these days in a lot of places what should be this totally normal reaction to pain is being rewarded.

But there's even more talk now about the ballsy, aggressive woman scrambling to climb the corporate ladder. Well, this woman is all about the *animus*.

Men who are aggressive and edgy in business are respected. Women who are aggressive and edgy tend to be frowned on. Still!

So it would appear that society has decided, at least for now, that we all have another side, but it isn't always okay to show it!

In any case, many times I'll be doing a reading and I'll realize that the King I'm seeing in a woman's cards is really her masculine side. And so I know that she needs to express this more. Maybe she needs to play hardball at work more. Maybe it means she needs to use the brain she was born with more. Maybe it means she needs to think more and feel less. Maybe she needs to be more decisive and firm.

Of course, when this happens it can cause huge confusion, because a reader doesn't know, for example, if that King is an actual guy or the other side of the female client.

Well, all I can say is that this animus/anima thing doesn't happen often, and for sure it won't come up for you for quite a while. But it just might at some point when you're good enough to spot it. And so I'm telling you here that it might. Again, relax. Tarot will advance only as fast as you can! And this incredible subtlety will make itself known to you only after you've done enough work that your right (psychic) brain is sufficiently developed.

Couples

A King and a Queen side by side will usually be a couple. If they're both of the same suit, I can be pretty sure they're a compatible couple.

But if the King is upside down and the Queen is right-side up, right away I know there's something wrong between them. And if they're back to back, well, then I get the immediate sense of two people turning away from each other in bed and in life. They're just not on the same page.

Again, this is something you can see quickly. It may take longer, though, to understand all the permutations.

For example, if you have the King of Swords upside down next to (or near) the Queen of Cups right-side up, you wouldn't want to be that woman. Think: a critical guy next to a sweet woman? Ugh.

Or maybe you see the Page of Cups upside down next to (or near) the Queen of Swords upside down, and you can imagine this sweet child doesn't stand a chance in the hands of this negative, critical woman/mother.

The Page of Cups

At some point after I'd been reading a while, I realized that this particular "child" card showed up in my readings most of the time to describe my client. My *adult* client.

As time went on, I discovered that the Page of Cups right-side up is a client who is emotionally healthy and has no psychological problems, no unresolved baggage to mess up a relationship. This person has probably been through psychotherapy.

The Page of Cups reversed, though, is another story. This is somebody who wasn't loved when little the way he or she needed to be by the mother, and if it shows up this way in a reading I always suggest that my client consider psychotherapy to deal with all that old pain.

Also, sometimes next to a Page of Cups reversed I'll see violence (the Five of Swords reversed) or seduction (the Knight of Cups reversed), and I'll know that something very bad happened to this little kid long ago.

But sometimes, of course, the Pages are actual kids, maybe children of the client. And sometimes that Page of Cups reversed is the child of the person sitting across from you.

Of course, it's hard to tell a client, "It doesn't look like your child is getting the love he/she needs from you." But I do it, because I'm all about protecting children.

Again, none of this will occur for you if you don't come from the place I do in terms of psychology. But if you do have a deep interest in mental health, please keep this phenomenon in mind for when you get good enough to spot it and use it in a healing way.

Knights

It took me years to boil down the meanings of the Knights to single words or a concept each. Usually, this is the way the Knights appear in my readings now. Sure, they can also be young men and young women, but usually they appear to provide description.

In my readings a Knight concept can add huge shades of meaning, depending on which cards are added to make a complete sentence or thought. So learn the meanings and see how the Knights show up when *you're* doing readings. My students seem to have the most trouble understanding the Moon and the Knights, as I did. So my only suggestion is to keep reading real people using my definitions until you can see *your own* pattern of meaning for these cards.

If you don't come up with anything of your own, that's fine too.

Right-Side-Up Court Cards

Court Cards and certain of the Major Arcana that are right-side up will usually have a more positive meaning for the client than reversed ones. For example, an Emperor right-side up could be a CEO favorably disposed to you. An Empress right-side up is at least attempting to live up to her idea of a good wife/mother.

What Happens If You Run Out of Court Cards

If you're doing a reading and the story is really complicated (the client has a lot of people in his or her life), you may have all the Court Cards on the table but the story still isn't finished.

When this happens, I find other cards stepping in. I might see a King of Swords reversed husband, but the wife shows up as the Nine of Swords. Clearly, he's not nice and she's in sorrow. This can take a while to figure out, but it can be done. All of a sudden, one day you're doing a reading and you see it clearly. The Nine is *not* only about pain now, it's suddenly also representing the woman in pain next to the man who is causing it.

You know, I'm continually astonished at the capability of tarot to inform and to teach.

Sometimes I think it's just miraculous. And never can I explain it. So I take tarot and my work on faith. And maybe someday, if I'm meant to, I'll figure out the rest.

Reversed Card Meanings

I can't tell you how many readers don't use the whole pack of cards, or they only use the cards right-side up. This will work only so far. I mean, the Devil is malignant or dangerous or chronic when it's right-side up, but the Devil reversed is healthy and good. The Star right-side up is beautiful; reversed, it's depression. The Two of Cups reversed is two people *out* of love.

So if you don't learn the meanings of the reversed cards, then when they fall upside down there's absolutely no way you'll be able to do the kind of work you're reading this book to achieve. Tarot cards were *designed* for this. So just do it. Learn everything. Have the tools you need. Would you try to fix a car with three wrenches and no screwdriver?

No kidding.

The same goes for using only the Major Arcana to do readings. As I said, these cards deal with the large and overriding issues in a person's life, but without the Minor cards you're probably not going to get any useful information about the day-to-day things and decisions, which is what we're confronted with most of the time. We live day to day. We have to decide things every day. So a competent reading must deal with the day-to-day, and the Major Arcana cards alone were never designed to do this.

The Gay Client

In 1948, sex researcher and author Alfred Kinsey announced that 10 percent of the US male population was gay. But in a 2017 Gallup poll, 4.5 percent of adult Americans identified as LGBT.

I myself find that gay clients seek me out often, but not spectacularly so. I believe it's because these people are artists at heart and find my method (and my vibe?) compatible with their own instincts.

So now I need to explain something. There is no particular card in tarot to represent homosexuality, despite the percentages being thrown around.

So this is what happened for me in this regard. After reading people for a while, I started to notice that a particular Queen kept showing up when the client was a gay male and a particular King kept showing up when the client was a gay female. And this has held true for my entire career. The same two Court Cards. After I thought about it for a while, I realized that these two particular cards have meanings that I both consciously and probably *unconsciously* associate with gayness. In fact, I learned something about my own unconscious attitudes from doing tarot! Nothing bad—just the way my own mind works and how I "see" people and their roles in life.

So I suggest that every time you read for a gay male, make a note of what card comes up; I'm 99 percent sure it'll be the same card every time. The same will be true if you work with a gay female. If you pay attention, eventually you'll know which two cards represent gayness to *you*.

And this is why I won't reveal my "gay" cards. They might not be relevant to *your* life, your attitudes, or your thinking. But if you do ascertain which cards signify gayness to you, it will never change.

Further, while I realize there are many transgender people out there, so far not one transgender individual has sought me out. I believe this is because the issue is far from my own concerns and history. The people who seek me out tend to be addicts, executives, and healthcare professionals, among others. As a result, I've had little chance to chart what cards come up for me with the transgender segment of the population.

Actually, I wish somebody with this kind of experience would write a book about it. It would interest me a lot.

CHAPTER 5
PRACTICAL TAROT APPLICATIONS

As I mentioned earlier, in the right psychic hands, a tarot card can be as clear an indicator as a fingerprint when it comes to crime. In medicine, it can be the mystical equivalent of an X-ray. When it comes to money, it can be the financial adviser some of us so desperately need. In this chapter I go into some detail about my experiences using tarot to investigate crime, encourage healing, and help guide my clients' thinking about money.

Crime

Late in the 1980s I was privileged to meet through a mutual friend a homicide detective with the New York Police Department. His terrible, dark place was the world of murdered children and their killers. Twice he came to me, case cold, with no definitive information and no more leads. I had to know he was desperate; psychics are always a last resort, if they are resorted to at all. But this man knew me, so he trusted me.

In the first case, a twelve-year-old girl had been assaulted and murdered. The detective asked me if I could "see anything." That night I tried to make myself quiet and laid out the cards for this little girl. I didn't understand what

I was seeing, but that night as I slept, I saw a man clearly in a dream. His head was practically shaved and he was stuffing clothes into a dark blue duffel bag. Even in the dream, I knew it was the girl's killer.

The next day I called the detective and told him, "I had a dream." I described the man and what I saw him doing. The detective said, "That's him. That's our prime suspect. He just joined the navy." The detective had needed some kind of confirmation that he was on the right track—how else to do it without evidence?—and I was able to give him that confirmation.

So in this case what I was able to do was confirm the identity of the suspect. For sure this information had come to me from the cards, though not from the reading directly. It had planted itself in my subconscious and then showed up in this dream. Why didn't I see this guy when I was awake? Because I get really upset about child killings, that's why. So it's very hard for me to stay objective.

In a second case involving another young girl who had disappeared, I again got "good" information and the detective was grateful because it seems that something I said put him on a new path.

I have to say that not all police officers are willing to consult with psychics. Who can blame them? There are so many frauds out there and there's so much on the line! So I was grateful for this chance to do that work and actually help. That cop who reached out to me is a brave man in far more ways than one.

Finally, as for the power of oracles in solving crime, I can point to Elizabeth Smart, the girl who was held hostage for months in Utah. I used the *I Ching* for this, asking the question "Why did she disappear?" For the answer, I received the hexagram called "the Marrying Maiden," which basically has to do with a man coming along and asking for the hand of a woman in marriage. I thought I must be totally off base. I mean, she was just a kid. Marriage? But what did we learn had happened to Elizabeth Smart? A crazy guy had come along and stolen her to be his "wife."

Once again, the *I Ching* was exactly right. And I was completely wrong not to trust what it was telling me. I let logic, my *left brain*, think me out of what my psychic/right brain was telling me. I mean, the truth just didn't make sense. Now I know better.

And here I need to say something important. I would never have been able to do any of the crime work I'm talking about here if I hadn't spent many years before that working with tarot and developing my right brain, my psychic ability. And if I didn't have that investigator muscle to begin with, forget it. This is a powerful combination. I'd love to teach cops. Imagine what they could do with a bunch of picture cards.

Medicine

No, I don't use oracles to practice medicine. It's against the law to practice medicine without a license in the first place. But over the years I *have* been blessed to do some tremendous healing work using cards. As a matter of fact, I'm told there's a doctor at New York University Hospital here in Manhattan who refers patients to me occasionally when the medical staff are stumped.

This aspect of my career came to me in the form of a sweet young Irish girl named Molly who was having trouble holding down a job because of her "hands." She said they didn't "work right all the time." Using tarot, I thought I was looking at a brain tumor. I asked if she'd had any kind of brain scan. She said no. I asked if she had a neurologist (because I thought I was looking at an incompetent surgeon). She said yes, she had a neurologist. I said, "I'm urging you to have a brain scan—and if your current doctor won't do it, get rid of him and find somebody who will. Just know *you will be fine* if you do this." Because that was what I saw for her outcome: Temperance (being fine) and the Magician (the great healer).

After this I had no activity in the medical arena. Nobody came to me with an issue. Six months later, though, Molly got in touch with me. She wanted me to know she'd taken my suggestion to heart and found a new neurologist. The new doctor had done the brain scan, found the tumor in her brain, and removed it.

And she would live.

I was in awe, really. We can do *this* with tarot? Who knew?

Since then I've found many things through my work having to do with health and healing. I've been able to identify many health issues for both people and animals. I've even been able to make suggestions as to how exactly to improve a bad diet when illness threatens. But in *every* case, first I lay out the situation and *then* I urge the client to see a doctor.

See, as I said, my job is to add new information to existing information so proper decisions can be made. I'm not the answer. I'm only one of the answers. If I'm lucky, that is.

And this is a funny story. After many years of being aware of and promoting the work of medium Jeffrey Wands, I finally went to see the man late in 2017, not to connect with people I'd lost but more to confirm things I thought I'd learned along the way.

In the process of me telling him what I do, I mentioned that I'd been able to use tarot to diagnose illness.

And *he* said, "Well, don't get too carried away with yourself about it. *He's* doing the diagnosing." Apparently, a brilliant surgeon and cancer researcher and a dear friend who had died in the mid-eighties was standing behind me during the session, and Jeffrey was referring to him! I started laughing and thanked my friend Angelos for helping me in my work. (See? As it says in the Bible, "I can of my own self do nothing.")

Here are some things I've come across so far in a pioneering sort of way when it comes to medicine.

In the mid-nineties, using tarot, I discovered a causative link between breast cancer and repressed anger (the Moon and the Five of Swords reversed). Then, maybe ten years later, I happened to read in the paper about that very finding by researchers. As reported by the *Journal of Psychosomatic Research*, these included scientists at King's College Hospital in London, the University of Rochester, and the Harvard School of Public Health, among others. Just as I am, these researchers are deeply interested in the connection between cancer and suppressed emotion.

So starting in the mid-nineties, even before the professionals made the discovery, I'd *already* been able to encourage women to see both a gynecologist and a psychotherapist: one to deal with the breast and one to deal with the anger. Because I've also learned that if we don't deal with this kind of lifelong, buried, under-the-surface anger, it'll just show up in the body in some other way. Sadly, you can pretty much count on it. And maybe this explains relapse when it comes to cancer. Cancer may be just the *symptom* and not the whole actual disease.

Likewise when it comes to addiction. I think it's because I have addiction in my own extended family that I've always attracted a lot of addicts—alcoholics, narcotics users, compulsive gamblers, obese people, chain smokers, workaholics—all of whom use the addiction to anesthetize themselves from the emotional pain they've been carrying around since early childhood. Here I recommend that a client join a support group to encourage abstinence *and* start seeing a psychotherapist to uncover and eradicate the terrible pain that makes addicts need so badly to anesthetize themselves in the first place.

I have to tell you, my discoveries about addiction may be unorthodox, but I *see* everything. I see the pain. I see who caused the pain. I see when it started. I see how very young the person was at the time the pain started (always very young). And I can assure you that there are only a few out there now treating addiction from this very perspective. (John Bradshaw comes to mind as one of these. He's an amazing man with a great gift. His work with addicts, his books and videos, I will always be able to recommend. They will stand the test of time, because he is rooted in truth.)

So bottom line, if you have the disease of alcoholism (the Devil, Temperance reversed, Strength reversed), while you need support not to drink, AA won't be enough to heal the pain that drove you to *start* drinking. The same is true for obesity (the Devil, Temperance reversed, Justice, Strength reversed), compulsive spending (the Devil, the Six of Pentacles), and compulsive gambling (the Devil, the Seven of Swords, the Six of Pentacles right-side up or reversed).

I'm going to go into a lot of detail in this book about card combinations. For now it's enough to tell you that the appearance of the Devil can make an otherwise relatively harmless thing a malignant thing. So pay attention to it.

Can people do this kind of thing with tarot cards, or any oracle for that matter, with only a little bit of study and work? No, I don't think so. I know there are people out there charging money to teach tarot in a weekend. Well, they may be teaching, but who'll be learning? It's all just too much to absorb.

And look, maybe you'll never be able to do crime and/or healing work well, but that'll just be because they're not high on your list of priorities, interests, or talents to start with. Maybe you're financially savvy instead. Maybe you're a dancer, a writer, a painter.

Still, I want all my students to know all the possible applications of the oracles, to be aware that this stuff is out there in case there's an interest. For now, it's enough to know that you can learn most of what I know, if only because I can teach it. And I know you can do that because my students are doing it.

So please, just don't get demoralized and down and quit if it takes longer than you think it "should." I didn't really "get" algebra until I was fifteen. Then, out of nowhere, it all fell into place. But you can imagine how I felt at fourteen.

So what I've learned is that my students learn and grow at their own pace. If I see them progressing from one stage to another, that's all that matters to me. The fact is that we all learn and grow at our own pace. Why should this field of mine be an exception?

So if it's slow going, just banish discouragement right here and now! Just get it out of your vocabulary. If you care, if you try, if you work at it, you will learn. Take pride in that.

Money

This brings me to a recent experience. One of my longtime students called to ask me my opinion. One of her friends, who dowses, advised her to move her savings from one investment firm to another. (Dowsing, I then learned, is the art—not the science—of using a pendulum to arrive at answers to questions. It may derive from long ago when dowsers used willow branches to find water deep in the earth. If the forked branch dipped, there was probably water down there. There's probably a scientific reason for why this works.)

But to give financial advice using a pendulum? I have to tell you, I basically freaked.

Look, never, ever, ever make a financial decision based on what a psychic *thinks* is happening. Never. No matter how the psychic arrives at the information. And never be the one to give such advice unless you happen to be a psychic *and* a financial planner.

See, when it comes to money, as with medicine, you have to be totally *practical* first.

So I asked this student of mine who'd gotten the advice: "Do you have all your money with the broker with whom you've entrusted your money? How long has this firm been investing your money? How did you hear about this broker? Has the broker lost any of your money so far? Has the broker outperformed the stock market so far? How long has the broker been in business? Who founded the company? In what stocks or funds does the fund invest? Does that firm speculate? Has the firm or the broker faced criminal investigation or charges? And please tell me you have at least *some* of your money somewhere else."

Of all of this, my student could tell me only that the new firm had had her money for six months and that she had "a little more" in a bank.

And, oh my god, it also turned out that, based on the recommendation of a man *she didn't even trust in other things*, she had in fact put most of her life savings in the hands of this company she herself knew nothing about.

Talk about a disaster waiting to happen.

When I got upset on her behalf, she finally admitted that she would "just sleep better at night" if she knew her money was in the hands of a different firm, in a retirement fund that I myself happened to know to be (so far at least) a *conservative, careful* money manager. That is, I knew it to be a good firm—*not* based on some oracle in the hands of somebody with little or no skill, but *based on the track record and reputation of the firm*. And based on this *only*.

So I suggested that she consider moving her money to this retirement fund while keeping something in the bank, maybe in CDs. And if I hadn't recognized the name of the fund she mentioned, I would've also suggested that *she* do some research on it, asking the money managers there the questions I was asking her. In fact, I suggested she do this anyway, so she could be in *charge* of her money.

Finally, I told this woman that *never* should a reader give financial advice without having actual basic information, training, and a track record *as a financial adviser*. Well, at least this student has learned a good lesson in what *not* to do when she starts working with the public. And then I referred her to Suze Orman's books for solid, safe information on where women can put their money, when it's best to do so, and why.

All this is here in such detail because if you plan to be a professional reader, somebody like this will walk through your door some day and you'll have to have the courage to tell the person you can't help them, in detail, with what they're thinking about because you're just not familiar enough with the world of finance and investment.

In fact, there's never a case like this when I don't refer people to the professionals trained to handle this crucial area of life.

In the Arts

Here, again, when a client came to me one day, another whole new world was revealed to me. I'd been working professionally for about four years when a guy in his mid-twenties came for a reading. As is my usual practice, I laid out the cards and started talking. I guess I went on for about five minutes. When I finally came up for air, he said, "Yeah, that's the novel I'm writing. But what about my *life*?"

Holy smokes! It had never occurred to me (a writer myself) to use tarot as an idea generator. But clearly, if I could see what he had written, then the reverse had to be true. Since that time, whenever I'm stuck as to what a character of my own would do next, I do a spread and basically I take dictation! Through tarot, I always come up with things my own left brain could never have thought of (too focused), so I always get interesting twists. And everything I get is plausible! Yes, my character *would* do that, I realize. Amazing.

(There are those who think writers' characters are purely extensions of themselves. This is not always the case. If I use the tarot to understand a character better—maybe he's a serial killer—I'm sure not reading for *me*.)

Frankly, as far as I know, there's really no end to the *practical* uses of tarot once you're comfortable with reading and you're working to master the meanings of the cards, and once you're comfortable with working to explore and understand what you yourself are bringing to the party in terms of experience, opinions, attitudes, and aptitude.

For example, I've seen exploding tires in cards. I've seen brake-fluid leaks. I've seen politics in the workplace. I've seen the theft of intellectual property. It's *all* out there, if only somebody wants to find it. It's all useful. And it's all important to somebody's life out there.

CHAPTER 6

SPREADS

In this chapter I talk about laying the cards down on the table so they can be interpreted in a known *context*. In the same way that astrology labels the various houses of a chart (representing the body, values, communication, etc.), so too does tarot need something *known* to hang its hat on. That thing is called a *spread*. In this chapter I show you the spread I've used for decades and how it works.

There are a lot of spreads out there. There's the classic spread I talked about earlier, the Celtic Cross, which uses ten cards, and which I think is way too philosophical and nuanced for everyday work with clients who are just trying to handle day-to-day problems and issues. (See appendix 1 for more on this spread.)

And there are other, creative spreads I've come across, such as the three-card spread (past, present, future) and the astrological spread (twelve cards, one for each zodiac house; this spread is also described in appendix 1). And I'm sure there are others out there that have eluded me so far. But I've found that the spreads I've come across over the years just aren't good enough for the subtleties that arise in readings.

So, from early on I've used the seven-card spread I learned from Jeff Norman, who came along at exactly the right time (naturally). Mostly, this Catholic woman was impressed by the way this man literally handled the cards. He wasn't afraid of them. He didn't treat them like God made them. He didn't treat them like they came from hell. He simply used them the way you'd use a wrench or a screwdriver or a dish towel. Cards as tools.

Also, at that time I was trying to conquer my conditioned fear of tarot. (Catholics like me tend to be excommunicated from the Church for "dealing with the devil.") And despite the much-vaunted suggestion that we readers should kind of "worship" cards, I could see that in his hands they *were* just a tool. Just to be clear: Tarot cards have no power in and of themselves. They're not magical. They're simply an extension of the brain. (For this reason, I don't care if the client touches the cards or not. I don't care which hand the client uses. The cards simply do what we ourselves are able to do. Nothing more, nothing less.)

So after seeing Jeff work on TV week after week, my fear of tarot dissipated and my spread of choice for working with clients became his seven-card spread. This has become the one I teach.

The thing about this spread is it's like an armature in the hands of a sculptor. An armature is a crude wire structure used to hold clay. It defines the basic shape (say, the human body), but it doesn't dictate the details. So the same armature can be used for the clay sculpture of a man or a woman (and probably a tall child).

Likewise, the seven-card spread creates limits and structure, but there's also a lot of leeway in there for getting creative. (This is not so true of the Celtic Cross.)

So, for a reader, the spread is basic operating procedure. And I have to say that I've found my spread, with its structure and wide-open parameters, to be almost as important as the cards themselves. If we have some kind of structure, we're not going to go off in all kinds of directions and on all kinds of tangents. There is the issue: the first card. There is the outcome: the seventh card. There are the ameliorating influences, the background, the things going on simultaneously and in the past, reflected by the other cards.

As you look at the spread examples that follow, when card names are given, take your pack and find those cards and lay them down in the order I show here so you can see what the heck I'm talking about.

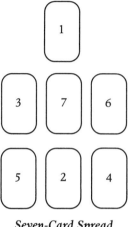

Seven-Card Spread

In the seven-card spread, the first card identifies the *issue*. The seventh card tells us the *outcome*. Cards 2 through 6 elaborate on various aspects of the life or the problem at hand. The diagram above shows the sequence used in laying down the seven cards.

Now here's what I've discovered. If you lay seven cards on the table and nothing else, you won't really have much of an idea of what's going on. Say the Ace of Swords is card 7. And it means: making a decision. Well, I'm going to want to know *what* decision. For those not using my method, there's a lot of guesswork here and just as much room for error. For example:

1
Ten of Cups
reversed

card 3   7   card 6
Ace of Swords

card 5   card 2   card 4

If card 1 is the Ten of Cups reversed (broken marriage) and card 7 is the Ace of Swords (a decision), I need to be able to tell my client what decision will be made. Is the client going to decide to leave? Is the client going to decide to stay? I never say what decision "should" be made, because who am I to give anybody advice? So I'd simply have to tell my client, "The way things stand now, if you do A and B, you'll end up with C."

But with my system, I'm able to come up with exact, detailed information by *adding* cards to the basic seven to tell me *more* about the basic seven.

In our example, say I add a card to the Ace of Swords and it turns out to be the Ten of Pentacles; and I add another card and it turns out to be the Six of Swords reversed—then I know the person will choose to stay in the broken marriage, at least for a while, because there's financial security in it.

1
Ten of Cups
reversed

card 3	7	card 6
	Ace of Swords	
	Ten of Pentacles	
	Six of Swords	
	reversed	
card 5	card 2	card 4

The thing here is that many times people simply need affirmation that the conclusion they've come to is the best they can do at the moment.

Now read this section again, look at the cards on your table, and think about how this all works.

Are All the Cards in a Spread Equally Important?

No, not all of them. But the first and the seventh cards? Absolutely.

I'm at the point now where sometimes a card shows up only because it contains a detail I need to know. On the card in the Rider-Waite deck, the Fool carries a white flower. Maybe the card shows up because it's the white flower that's important. How do I know if it's the detail or the whole card that I need to pay attention to? I just seem to know. But, for sure, I couldn't do this at first! Over the years of working, though, I've become able to do it. I have developed my right brain for so long that it just seems to take over. And things, as I've said, "occur" to me.

For your purposes as a student, though, each card will always mean the face value. The whole card and nothing else will matter. And you'll be able to do good work. As you progress, though, other things will start to happen. But not until you're ready.

So for the seven-card spread, cards 1 and 7 will *always* be more important than the others.

Also, sometimes I'll be doing a reading and a card will simply *seem* to be larger or taller or somehow in the air above the table. So I go with that and emphasize the meaning of that card. (A VERY big father and a VERY little boy beside him, for example, is what it *feels* like to me.) One of my students who's been working on this stuff for ten years has started to be able to experience this sensation once in a while.

The same goes for using only the Major Arcana to do readings. As I've said, these are the large and overriding issues in a person's life, but without the Minor cards you're probably not going to get any information that is at all *useful* about day-to-day things and decisions. And we live day to day, right? We have to decide things every day. So a competent reading must deal with the day-to-day, and the Major Arcana were never designed to do this.

Feeling the Cards

When I started studying tarot, I acted out a lot of the images. For the Two of Swords, for example, I crossed my arms tight across my chest and tried to see how that *feels*. As you progress as a reader, these feelings will make themselves known somehow inside of you, but I think it can't hurt to know what the physical images are trying to convey.

Now look at the Three of Swords. What does it *feel* like? This will probably be harder because there's no person on that card. But try this anyway at least once with all the cards. The Nine of Swords is a weeping woman. I showed this card to my four-year-old niece once and asked what she saw. She said, "The woman is crying." Yes, she is.

As I said earlier, the tarot cards most currently in use today were designed by people who thought hard about the *implications* of the pictures. And so the Nine of Swords woman is indeed weeping—rivers of tears, in fact—so we know when we see it that somebody is, was, or will be in grief about something.

CHAPTER 7

How to Study

In this chapter I teach you how to study and work with tarot cards in such a way that you don't overwhelm yourself. This is how I developed my system. This is how I teach my students. It's step by step. And I ask that you study an hour a day, every day, if you can.

Before You Start

There are three things you need to know before you start.

First of all, here is a good story. I have a really intuitive student who has no interest at all in healing, though in life she is a "helper." Early on, using the pack I use, she started *feeling* as if certain cards were higher on the table than the others, fatter than the others, thinner than the others. From this she would feel that certain things were true—and she'd be right! I'm so envious of this woman, who could do this practically from the start, even with health issues! It was many years before this started happening for me.

The second thing to know is that you need to be willing to be patient. It takes a while to become a good (truly helpful) reader. And it might take even longer for most people to become confident readers.

The third thing to know before you start is that your own symbolism will start showing up at some point, and that's when you start adding what you already know to what I'm telling you here.

A reading is only as good as what a reader brings to it. So the more you know going in, the better you'll be. No guesswork about it!

Start Small

Okay, so now here's what you need to do every day, for as much time as you can give it:

Practice combining cards. And read what you see aloud.

Take a basic card and put another card beside it. Say aloud the combined meaning.

I'd like you to start with the Page of Rods/Wands (*talking about*). Put it on the table.

Next to the Page, put another card. Just draw one at random.

Let's say you draw the Seven of Cups. So now you have the Page of Rods/Wands (*talking about*) + the Seven of Cups (*dreams*). Together those two cards say: *talking about dreams*.

Say this ALOUD.

Now keep the Page, remove the Seven, and add another card. Keep replacing the second card, each time saying aloud: *talking about* _____.

Now try the High Priestess (*the ideal*). Put a card next to it. Suppose you draw the Three of Pentacles (*skilled job*). What do you have? *The ideal skilled job*. Go through the whole pack again.

Then start in with a new base card and add the other cards to it.

Once you can whip through these, even with the definitions in the book in front of you, feel free to use a base card and add *two* cards each time.

Then three cards.

The whole idea here is to start learning how to combine concepts the way we do when expressing complete thoughts: *yellow + house = yellow house*.

I have a student now who's been working at this for only a short while and she's up to four cards and very excited about all the information to be found there. She has worked as a psychic, but she could never be specific and in control of what she was doing, and she hated herself for it. Now she's learning how to do this and she's, well, over the Moon about it.

Telling Stories

Let's say a reporter is walking down the street and comes upon the scene of a fire.

He pulls out his notebook and starts asking questions: "What happened? Do you know how the fire started? Do you know where it started? Is anybody hurt? What hospital did the victims go to?" And by asking all kinds of questions like this, the reporter puts together the story of that fire.

Your job as a card reader is to *ask yourself* the same types of questions as you draw cards to respond to your client. I say throughout this book that a good reader doesn't have to rely on intuition alone. God gave your brain two hemispheres. Use them!

On the other hand, if you're the rare reader who is gifted enough to do all the work purely by intuition, that's wonderful!

There's a rather famous psychic detective named Dorothy Allison who was able to "see" things—specific things, places, signs, vehicles—purely through intuition. She helped the police find missing murder victims and their killers. Well, hers was an incredible gift, miraculous really. But most of the rest of us psychics aren't so blessed. Sometimes we mere mortals need to rely on all our senses in addition to psychic ability.

So to do a good reading, we need to ask ourselves questions, and draw cards to answer those questions. And then we can tell our clients complete stories: stories that have a beginning, middle, and end. Who, what, when, where, why, how.

Say you're reading a client with job problems. Well, maybe there is one *big* story that started way back when, when the person made what seemed to be even a small decision and it ended up impacting his life to this day. (For example, say the client chose a certain career and is no longer happy with it.)

Well, if you're going to be any help at all, you need to be able to tell the client when something started, what's going on now, and where the situation is heading, so the client can see the beginning and attempt to understand the old motives versus the new. You need to be able to explain what the client can do now to change direction a bit, to diversify, or to make a completely new choice. I see myself as a namer of options and outcomes: *If you do this, you can expect that.*

For example, rape victims are sometimes counseled to think back to the day of the attack and remember what exact decision was made that started the chain of events that led to the rape. Maybe it was as simple as deciding to walk home one lovely night instead of taking the bus. This is not done to blame the victim! It's done to reassure the victim that in order for something like the rape to happen again, a tremendous number of little things would have to happen *in just the right order* to put the person in the wrong place at the wrong time again.

So, say you're reading for a client who chose to be a doctor because the men in his family *always* become doctors. You see the father expecting it of his son (the Emperor); you see the son not being listened to (the Page of Rods/ Wands reversed); you see that the guy is a good doctor (the Magician) but unhappy (the Three of Swords) despite the money he makes (the Six of Pentacles).

So now you can tell him his issue goes beyond not liking his career. You can suggest that his choice in the first place seems to have had something to do with a fear of displeasing his father way back when. So you take him back to when he used to talk about *his own* dreams and was ignored, when he was a kid. Now your client can start to see his current issue in terms of the *larger* picture of his whole life. It can become clear to him that if he chooses to leave medicine, he may be risking the wrath or rejection of his father. Only he can decide if this matters anymore.

And then you line up as many cards as it takes to see what can happen if he does choose to stop being a doctor.

Whatever shows up, you can now tell a story with a beginning, middle, and end. This is typical of my readings. I try to find the whole enchilada. I do it so people can make choices and decisions without lacking pieces of important information.

And if you start reading cards like you're reading these sentences, you can do this too.

And now for a very serious subject that I'd be remiss if I didn't go into here.

Understanding Timing

In addition to doing the "flashcard" thing, running through the pack with one base card and all the others following, I'd like you to start using the seven-card spread to read actual people. Famous deceased people are optimal. You can always google the facts after you've looked at their lives with cards, and then you can compare what you think you've found with what actually was. Do these readings aloud, too.

Now, in an actual reading, timing can be crucial. Everybody wants to know *when*, and way too often I cannot answer that. It's not my thing. I see what and who, but I rarely see when, even when I'm looking for it.

Astrology is the science that deals with timing things. Of all the oracles, astrology in the right hands can give optimum results. With tarot I've been able to do a lot: predicting exact days, months, seasons. But this comes from *feelings* combined with a general knowledge of planetary transits rather than from fact. And so I know it's unreliable and I can't be teaching it.

Still, I'm offering here what I feel when it comes to timing. Over the years I've come upon a few devices that can make some timing less difficult to convey: a kind of timing *shorthand* as it relates to specific cards.

So pay special attention to mastering these shorthand meanings for the following cards:

- Use the Knight of Swords to mean: out of the blue, suddenly
- Use the Eight of Rods/Wands to mean: any minute now; *reversed:* not any minute now
- Use the Ten of Rods/Wands to mean: eventually
- Use the Wheel of Fortune to mean: it's time to do something; *reversed:* it's not time
- Use the Four of Rods/Wands to mean: on hold; *reversed:* no longer on hold
- Use the Hanged Man to mean: hanging around, pending, waiting

Of course, most of my clients, when anticipating the arrival of love in their lives, tend to be rather impatient (to put it mildly). Nobody likes to hear, "Eventually he/she will come."

So I'm always busy looking to see what is to be done *in the meantime*.

And I'm *always* reassuring my clients, "Love comes when it's time. And nothing we can do will make it happen faster. So just live and love your life the best you can until that moment." For this I usually point to Barbra Streisand, my personal icon for love coming when it's time. I believe she met James Brolin when she was fifty-four.

In the meantime, I never lie. So if I don't see it, I don't see it. And I don't pretend I do.

Always be honest. A lot of times people don't want to hear unpleasant stuff (though of course they do, deep down, or they wouldn't be sitting across from me), but it's my job as a reader to tell them, in as kind and compassionate a way as I can. Likewise, I keep tissues on my table, because some readings can produce real feelings, and sometimes these are the first real feelings the client has *ever* let himself or herself have about somebody or something that's caused real pain for a long time.

And this, too, is about timing. If I see something, I know it's time for the client to hear it. In my entire career, this approach has never been wrong.

So if somebody asks you in particular for a reading, it's a good bet it's because they need to hear what you, in particular, have to say. So make it good, make it honest, make it thorough, and make it as clear as possible.

Choosing a Significator

This section refers to your experiments with actual readings of actual people.

In most books on tarot, you will find the author asking you to choose a "significator," especially with the Celtic Cross spread. The significator is the card chosen to represent the client in the reading. You're asked to put it on the table first.

Well, now I'm asking you: please don't. And this is why.

Say your client is a woman, and one of you chooses the Queen of Cups for her and puts it on the table as the significator. Now this card is no longer *available* to show up at some other point if it's needed. It's no longer going to show up to tell you something you really need to know about your client's emotional makeup.

The Queen of Cups reversed is a woman who settles, who sells herself short, who doesn't put a high enough price on herself. But it may be *crucial* to learn this about your client from a spread. Maybe she's staying in an abusive marriage or maybe she's in a terrible job. But how can you know it's because she sells herself short if the card is out of play? It's like trying to play solitaire with fifty-one cards or finish a jigsaw puzzle with a piece missing. We can't ever have a complete picture about a client if a critical card is already being used for no reason at all.

Bottom line, if you're doing a reading and this Queen shows up, it tells you that you're dealing here with your client's emotions, self-image, self-love, self-esteem (as opposed to career, for example). And if this card shows up reversed in somebody's cards, it usually means that the woman is settling because she doesn't believe she deserves better than what she has.

So when I realized how crucial it is to have *all* the "people" cards available to tell me a client's complete story, that was the day I stopped using a significator. You can do it, of course, but I assure you that something really important will eventually be missing from a reading.

Be Consistent in Your Movements

Do this:

Put your cards on the table in front of you upside down. Now take a card and turn it over. It doesn't matter which card. I want you to notice exactly how you turned that card over. Left to right? Top to bottom? Bottom to top? Whatever you realize you just did, for the rest of your life, turn cards over the exact same way.

No, this isn't about any kind of magic or superstition. It's about making sure you never "cheat" because you want a certain card to fall a certain way. I mean, what would be the point of that? If you choose one method for turning over cards and stick to it, you can always trust what you see and you can't play games with the outcome.

CHAPTER 8

MY APPROACH TO CONTROLLING THE READING

In this chapter I talk about what I can and can't control in a reading. Mostly, what I can control easily is the cards chosen. What's harder, though, is dealing with the client who can't help trying to take charge. You'll experience this too if you work with the general public. Just try hard not to let these people run you.

Everything in Confidence

As soon as you start working in earnest with the public, you'll realize that you're being entrusted with incredible information—some of it damning, some of it wonderful, and most of it quite personal. Which means, in a nutshell, you can never, ever repeat to another person what transpires in confidence between you and a client during a reading.

In fact, I take it a step further: Nobody ever even knows who consults with me, not even the person who referred the client. If the client wants to tell, that's fine. But I don't say, and I won't say. To my mind, this would be a terrible betrayal. All of us are entitled to our secrets.

Likewise, with one exception in my entire career, nobody is present when I work except me and my client. This is because I can't ever guarantee what I'll see and how much the client wants to protect that information, and I can't do an honest, proper reading if I have to censor myself. So no audience allowed.

And there's a funny story here (well, maybe not so funny). I read for a married guy and saw he was having an affair. A week later he asked me if I'd read for his wife, in his presence. And it just came to me that this coward wanted *me* to deliver the news of his infidelity to his unsuspecting wife, through a card reading. I politely refused, and I made a mental note about *not* reading for both sides of any couple, even if it's months or years apart. Last I heard, the guy in question was still having the affair and still married.

Synchronicity

I can't stress this enough. You just can't let your client manage the card reading. If the client isn't in tune with what the *really* important thing is in his or her life at that moment, you'll be asked questions that don't get answered by the cards. At least not right away.

When this happens (which is a lot), what you'll see first of all is the answer to the *unasked* question. Sometimes it happens because the client is trying to pull an end run by evading the real issue. Sometimes the client just isn't aware that the problem is bigger than it seems. And most of the time the client is totally not interested in what you have to say. But this is what you're being paid for. So do the job.

An example is the client who comes asking about an optional job change when the fact is his or her marriage is falling apart. The cards I see first in this case will most likely show the dying relationship.

Then there are the clients who cannot sit still and hear bad stuff. I had a client once who was obsessed with getting married, but for years I just didn't see it happening. And so, many times this woman would listen to what I had to say and then start grabbing card after card in a kind of frenzy, as if she could *make* her desired answer happen.

When people do this, I just sit back until they're done. Then I suggest that they please go to psychotherapy, because their issue is not getting married, it's being obsessed with it to the point that they lose control.

Timing

Also, almost a hundred percent of the time, I refuse to read people again until three months have passed, or at least not until some of the major changes and actions they need to make have been made. This is because I work hard to discourage clients from depending on me, and I encourage them instead to feel capable enough to take charge of their own lives and make their own independent decisions and believe in themselves enough to do so.

Of course, if I were always available to everybody all the time, maybe I'd be rich by now. But I'm not available, and I refuse to be.

If somebody's so needy that they seek daily or even weekly readings, I have psychotherapists to recommend. Because it's either addictive behavior or obsessive behavior or bordering on it. And I don't respect any psychic who doesn't work this way.

Face it, if a reading about the future is correct, then things aren't going to "change," which tends to be why the first reading I do for a person is usually the richest, the most detailed, and usually the most accurate. But some clients hope and wish things will change. They keep pushing and asking the same question over and over. So you, the reader, have to be firm. "No," you have to say. "If *you* don't change things, they'll just stay the same. And so will the cards."

Now I will explain time when it comes to tarot, at least the way I understand it.

If for some unlikely reason I were to read a person three days in a row, I would likely see three different time frames. For example, on Monday I might see 2011. On Tuesday I might see 1999. On Wednesday I might see 1967. None of these is necessarily wrong, but it does seem that certain moments in time seem to resonate somehow with certain other moments in time. It's some kind of synchronicity that's at work here, I think. So getting verb tenses right in a reading can be a challenge. Which is why I read mostly in the present tense.

Are Clients (Are We) Self-Aware?

Of all the thousands of readings I've done, there have been only a few hundred in which the client was totally in touch with his or her life and therefore asked the exact right question *first*. These are the folks who know themselves and have their priorities straight. See, if they don't, the cards will rat on the people who are trying to hide, either deliberately or not, what's really going on and troubling them. It's my job to convince people that they have their priorities wrong.

And this I believe as well: People come to me specifically because they already know, deep down, what I'm going to tell them. I believe they seek me out to hear what I have to say. Something moves them in my direction. Look, I don't understand this, but I absolutely believe it to be true. Because too many times the reading turns out to be a turning point in the client's life, and I can actually see this in real time.

Not that the client always likes what I'm saying, but I myself accept on faith that it's my job to say it at that moment in time.

The same is true when it comes to seeing time. Every once in a while for a couple of years now I've been seeing a great romantic partner in the future of a particular client. This guy doesn't appear in every reading—because my client has a lot of things to do before being ready to meet him. So what usually shows up, in the months-apart readings, is all the stuff she has to deal with first, getting through that swamp I mentioned earlier. She hates it. She wants it yesterday.

So, does the periodic absence of the guy mean he doesn't exist? No. Does it mean the reading is wrong? No. It simply means that some points in time resonate with other points in time. Somehow. In a way I don't understand. So I try to explain this to the client when this happens. She shrugs. Eventually she comes back and asks again. But not right away. So this is fine. I just don't cave to her disappointment. I do the job she's paying me to do. Thankfully, she gets that.

Finally, when it comes to how often a client might have a reading, here's another story.

In the late nineties, I read for a Sagittarius woman for one hour, with everything recorded as usual. She asked me when she could come back. I told her it would have to be only when at least some of what I was seeing had come to pass. NINE YEARS LATER my phone rings. It's the woman. She says, "Everything you told me has happened in the last six months. So can I come back now?"

I had to laugh. What *possible* use can a reading be if everything was right but it was all that far off? I mean, nine *years*?

Since then I've noticed that when I'm reading Sagittarians (the sign of long distances), I tend to be able to see much further into the future, in general. I'm not sure why, but it's a definite pattern for me. Probably because it's in them, and I'm just getting what I get from them in the first place.

Now, see, this isn't something the reader can control. So if this is your experience as a client, just go with it. Clearly, this Sagittarius woman had no problem at all letting her life unfold over time. And I think that's just wonderful! It's healthy. It's not micromanaging. Rather, it's living a life based on faith and self-confidence and a willingness to just see what happens without fear. This is the best attitude.

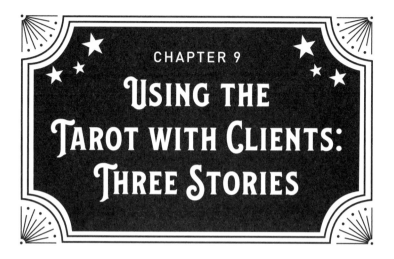

CHAPTER 9

USING THE TAROT WITH CLIENTS: THREE STORIES

I n this chapter I tell three stories. These are real situations brought to my table by three people whose identities are disguised. Who they are is in no way as important as what they were dealing with. These stories should help orient the student in terms of what can be done with tarot cards and real people and real situations.

Carla in "Love"

Carla is a woman in her early sixties. Her son has sent her to me in hopes I can "help" her (her word). She's clearly a well-bred woman, beautifully dressed, with lovely jewelry (including a wedding ring). She speaks with a slight accent.

I ask her to give me seven cards, face down and one at a time from a pile on the table. (I never shuffle. I just drop the cards on the table and mess them up with my hands.) Carla gives me seven cards. The first card will always be on top as I collect them in my hand, so there's no question of the order in which a client hands me the cards. This is crucial. The first card, remember, is the *issue*—what this spread is going to be about. And the first spread is usually the most important of the day. So when I have seven cards in hand, the first card will always be the top card.

As you read this text, find the cards I'm naming and, referring to the diagram on page 71, put them in front of you on a flat surface. Then read the text again.

The first card Carla hands me, the *issue*, is the **Four of Pentacles** (clinging in an unhealthy way to something).

The seventh card Carla hands me, the *outcome* of the first, is the **Six of Swords reversed** (not taking oneself out of a bad situation).

So I know already that Carla's issue here is she's hanging on to something that's bad, and she's choosing to stay in the situation.

The other five cards she's given me are the **Four of Rods/Wands reversed** (not a good home or work life); the **Knight of Pentacles reversed** (not able to stand one one's own two feet); the **Nine of Swords** (grief); **Temperance reversed** (depression); and the **King of Pentacles** (the provider, emotional and/or financial).

So the story as I see it so far? Somebody is clinging to a bad situation of some sort and making no effort to get away from it. Added to the scenario are a lousy home or work life, the inability to stand on one's own two feet, some kind of security issue, grief, and depression.

So I know already, just from these first seven cards, that if somebody's not able to stand on her own two feet, that person is bound to be insecure. And that insecure person is then at the mercy of whoever and whatever comes along. Wouldn't you be? I sure would. And so now I look at the **King of Pentacles** (for me, the archetypal provider) and I think: Is the person clinging to this man because he can provide and she doesn't feel she can stand on her own two feet? And I already know this insecurity may be totally emotional and having nothing to do with money.

But what I don't know right now is: What is the person clinging to? Is it Carla who's doing the clinging? Why isn't the person bailing on the situation? (Aha, probably too insecure to try?) Is it a bad home or work environment? (Sometimes it can be both, by the way.) And I'm already thinking I would be sad and depressed too if I were in this terrible spot. And now my feelings are totally engaged.

So next I do the most important thing I ever do in a reading: I start to identify what the first and seventh cards refer to, in specific, by drawing other cards to put on them.

Reading from left to right, I get:

On the clinging Four of Pentacles falls the **Ten of Cups reversed** (a bad marriage). So I know now that the clinging is connected to this marriage.

Then, on the Ten of Cups reversed falls the **Queen of Cups reversed** (a woman who doesn't feel she deserves better; she doesn't love herself). So I know now this self-defeating woman is connected to the bad marriage.

Then falls the **Three of Swords** (terrible pain). So I know now, if I didn't already, that there is pain connected to the woman and somehow to her marriage.

And because I want to be very sure what the source of the pain and the problem is, I take another card: I draw the **King of Rods/Wands reversed** (a man who's not committed to this relationship).

Now I say to Carla, "I'm seeing a woman in terrible pain, depressed, hanging on to a marriage that's really over, a marriage to a man who's not interested in commitment. Is that you?"

She tells me, "Yes, it's me. But is it really over?"

And at this, I realize why this woman is sitting at my table. Carla has some kind of dream or hope or wish that her failed marriage will somehow come back to life and be wonderful again. And she's hoping that I'll be able to tell her that.

But, see, what I also already know is that if the Ten of Cups is upside down, it's upside down. And from life itself we learn that unless *both* people want to try again to mend a broken relationship, it just can't happen. And if the King of Rods/Wands is reversed like this, this partner is no longer committed. So much for both people working together to save the relationship. This guy just doesn't want to, if he ever did.

I explain to Carla, "You're hanging on to a marriage that's over, to a man who's no longer committed to the marriage, and it hurts. I'm sorry. But you're wearing a wedding ring..." It was kind of a question. "He's still in the home?"

She says, "No, he left, but I keep thinking he'll come back. Won't he change his mind?" Well, I've heard this so many times from women it's just terrible. And my heart goes out to Carla for living in this painful fantasyland. Because, see, deep down we always know the truth. And I know that she does too. And I know it hurts like crazy.

So now I have to add, "Well, these cards are saying that you don't think you deserve better than this, Carla."

And I know also from experience that *from this one thing* I'm seeing the *root*, the seed of this entire disaster for this woman. She does not love herself. The Queen reversed tells me that Carla's in this boondoggle because she really doesn't feel she deserves better.

And so I also know now, from experience with tarot, that pretty soon the **Page of Cups reversed** will show up (the child not loved by the mother, when little, the way the child needed to be). The fact here is that unless these people go to psychotherapy, they always grow up to be folks who don't think they deserve what they dream of. I was one. I know.

Sure enough, this card falls later in Carla's reading. It falls atop the **Knight of Pentacles reversed**. (Why would a kid who's never been loved have any belief in herself? Why would she think she can make it on her own? She doesn't.) When this card does show up, I pick up both cards and show them to Carla, side by side, the Queen upside down and the Page upside down, and I say, "This is you now, and this is you when you were little. This child wasn't loved by her mom, so she grew up to be the woman who doesn't love herself."

And so now Carla starts to cry, not because I've hurt her but because it's true. And I'm so glad. For the first time in her life, this woman is letting herself *feel* some of the pain she felt when she was little and was basically rejected by her mother. This is the pain we bury at a very young age. This is the pain that comes back to bite us one day, inevitably. It's the pain that drives us all to therapy.

And so now I point to the wedding ring and say, "You know, you could take that off for a little while. When you leave today, you could just put it back on."

Carla thinks about it. She says, "You know, I've never taken it off."

But then, a miracle: She takes off the ring. And places it *very* carefully on the table. And that ring looks *enormous* there, even to me, this huge symbol of maybe years of suffering in Carla's marriage-that-wasn't.

Frankly, I'm shocked she's done it. But as I've learned over the years, people tend to find me when they're ready to hear what I have to say. And in many cases, the reading is the turning point in the person's life. Or so I often pray it to be.

Now think about it: we can see the roots of this woman's entire life *from only a few cards:*

Issue: The Four of Pentacles: next to this card, place the Ten of Cups reversed/the Queen of Cups reversed/the Three of Swords/the King of Rods/Wands reversed.

Outcome: The Six of Swords reversed.

(Please lay these cards out in this order and speak their meanings as if in a sentence. It is these sentences your clients will hear.)

So now I take a look at the **Six of Swords reversed**, the outcome. Carla's not taking herself out of this miserable situation. She's not even trying. In fact, she's admitting to me that she hopes this man—who is essentially gone in body if not in mind—will come back to her and the marriage.

I ask her, "Where's your husband now? The one who's not committed to your marriage?"

Carla tells me, "He left a few years ago. He's living with another woman. They have two kids."

Even as she's saying this amazing thing, her eyes are straying to that ring. And she adds, nodding, "He's not coming back, is he?"

I have to be logical here: the real issue is not the man! The *real* issue is this woman being willing to stay in this scenario this long, and why she would. See, we all make mistakes. But those of us who live in denial and stay there with some kind of false hope …

As Carla is asking if he's coming back, and already seeming to know he won't, I draw another card and put it on the Six of Swords reversed, the outcome. The card I draw is the **Eight of Cups** (denial, in this case). It's almost like arithmetic, once you realize how people tick. I tell her she's been in denial if she thinks he'll return if only she waits. More pain delivered by me. Then again, surgery hurts too.

I didn't know most of what I know now about human nature when I started with tarot. It's actually been the cards themselves and my clients who have taught me everything. And they continue to do so to this day.

So what Carla's been doing is refusing to admit what's right in front of her. Like many of us, she's been clinging to dreams that can't come true; she's been staying in a lousy situation because she keeps thinking things will get better.

But, see, there's just no magic. We're just telling ourselves stories to keep the pain away.

And once again my heart goes out to this woman. No wonder she's depressed and grieving. The marriage is dead. The woman who entered that marriage long ago has died, too. And she *knows* it, deep down. But she hasn't mourned any of that yet.

The other cards that fall on top of the first seven are important, but none of them are as meaningful as what I've covered here already. These things matter in the scenario, sure, but the root of the tree is the most important thing. If the root (issue) is diseased, so too will the tree (outcome) be diseased.

Carla's reading lasts for an hour.

And at the end of the hour I say, "You can put your ring back on now. It's okay if you want."

And Carla picks it up, that symbol of a lifetime of hurt. She considers it, she pushes it deep into her pocket, and she says, "I think I won't."

I could've cried for joy. This tremendous breakthrough! From a bunch of pictures on a bunch of pieces of cardboard and one incredibly courageous woman willing to see what she'd been deliberately blind to for years. Can you imagine?

Here is a footnote that is hugely important:

To understand the whole child-adult thing, you only have to remember that romance novel in which the mother is always involved with her own thing—with men, with work, with money worries, with an alcoholic husband, with whatever—and her child is always playing second fiddle. This is the exact child who'll grow up "thinking" she or he doesn't deserve to be first in anybody's heart.

I mean, *if my mom doesn't even care about me, what am I worth?* (This is the operating system that's driving us. And like a computer operating system, it too hums along in the background, invisible. And in this case, dangerous.) So, no, we're not aware of what's making us tick; we don't even know it's there. But it is what's driving us.

Just know this: We aren't born this way. We're *taught* this. We learn it. And we don't usually know that. And it happens to boys too. Many males just seem to cope better than females, diverting all their attention to work and career, or maybe to drugs or alcohol or gambling. Anything but deal with the pain. I feel really bad for guys, too. Admitting they need psychological help is to many of them an admission of weakness (when I know it to be an act of strength).

Also, this "thinking" we're not worth it? It's not a conscious thought, like "I think I'll go to the store." It's a *sub*conscious "thought," planted there by circumstances too early in life for us to remember. Such subconscious impulses can be really dangerous. A good reader inclined to this kind of perception will get it and be able to work with it. If you find this whole thing fascinating, then maybe you have the same "muscle" I do, which means a talent for this kind of psychological approach. If so, the clients who choose you will reinforce your sense that this may be your calling when it comes to tarot.

And one more thing on this subject: A client once accused me of having "mother issues" and attacking her mom because of it. I replied, "Neither my mother nor I was sitting at your dinner table when your dad was beating up on you kids and your mother wasn't lifting a finger to protect you."

She stared at me.

"And," I went on, "when your grandmother was neglecting your mom in the same way, we weren't there either." I explained, "This is totally not a judgment of mothers. It is a simple statement of fact. No man can serve two masters, and if a mother is afraid of abuse or is dealing with severe problems of all kinds, like your grandmother was, she will neglect the emotional needs of her own daughter. And so it goes."

My client nodded. It was all true.

See, the moms learn it from their moms, and so on back through history. The only way I know of to stop the cycle is to go to psychotherapy and relearn what we're all born knowing: we deserve to be loved; we deserve to be able to go after our dreams; we deserve to be able to dream in the first place the dreams we ourselves want to nurture and not pursue what others say we "should."

So then I asked this objecting client, again, to go to psychotherapy, if only because she was a single woman expecting a child herself and was obsessed with men. Well, that didn't look too good for the little kid she was going to have.

I've also found myself lecturing mothers at my table: "You have no right to do this to your children." They don't fight back. They nod. They *know*. I figure that if I see it, I have an obligation to the kids to say so and I'm *supposed* to. Look, I'm all about children: the ones we were and the ones inside of us when we're grown, but especially the ones we're going to give birth to. We owe them the best possible emotional foundation.

Joe and the Job

You know how some people come bouncing into a room, throw out their hand to shake, and are generally physically upbeat? Well, Joe isn't even close to that, despite the fact that I figure him for a guy in his late twenties. He's wearing clothes he might have slept in, his hair is mussy and askew, and he plops down in the chair I indicate and kind of collapses into it. Zero energy, zero enthusiasm—not even any obvious apprehension about this session, despite the fact this is the first time he's coming to see me.

As always, I ask Joe not to say anything until I've made my initial comments on the first cards. I ask for seven cards. Man, this guy is slooow. I start to wonder if he has an illness. I wonder if he's on some kind of heavy tranquilizer. I wonder…

This young guy has no energy *and* no affect (he seems not to be emotionally involved in what's about to happen). This can be good or bad. Acceptance is such a huge thing when one is getting a reading. And from his lethargic attitude, I figure him willing to accept everything I say.

These are the seven cards Joe gives me:

The *issue*, the first card, the point of view of the reading, is the **Ten of Pentacles** (security).

The *outcome*, the seventh card, is the **Eight of Pentacles reversed** (lack of a challenging job or no job at all).

So I can see that the priority in Joe's life right now is work, not in terms of success or enjoyment or promotion but rather of money, pure and simple. If there's no job or too low-level a job, how can we pay our bills? So these two cards alone are saying that Joe is facing a serious financial and work issue.

I tell him this. He says nothing. I'm not unnerved by the silence. A long time ago when I started working with people, if they didn't respond, it kind of undermined my confidence. After a while, I realized that not everybody is telling me I'm wrong by their silence. They're mostly life's listeners.

The next five cards are:

The **Star reversed** (depression); the **Two of Cups reversed** (no love being shared with another, or the end of a shared love); the **Three of Rods/Wands** (thinking about the next step in life); the **Seven of Cups** (dreams); and the **Emperor reversed** (domineering or bullying father or boss?).

But something doesn't fit right. I need more. I'm talking about *logic* here. How can this guy have dreams and be thinking about his next step in life if the real issue (the first card) is security and getting his bills paid and keeping a roof over his head? I mean, I don't see any kind of job-seeking behavior, at least so far. Add that to his total lack of energy ...

So right away I add a card to the Seven of Cups (dreams), and what falls is the **Four of Swords** (on hold, inaction). So now I see there's logic after all: whatever Joe's dreams may be, they're on hold for some reason. I'll be coming back to this after looking at the other cards.

I then add a card to the Three of Rods/Wands (again, *what* next step?). I mean, isn't Joe thinking about getting a job, a better job at least, to achieve some kind of security? Isn't that the next pragmatic step in this guy's life? See, I'm using my left brain here, trying to be as logical as I can. So I put a card on this next-step thing and it's the **Eight of Rods/Wands reversed** (something stalled, not happening, not going to happen, stagnation).

Aha, now I get it: his thinking about the next step is stalled.

This is on top of dreams on hold, in addition to no job or a lousy job, in addition to depression and no love relationship.

The poor guy.

Overall, I'm now getting a picture of inactivity. If I see the **Seven of Rods/Wands** (a résumé, fighting something with the advantage), then I can know the guy is trying, fighting. But this card never falls for Joe. Likewise, no **Five of Pentacles** (looking for a new job or a home—in this case it would be a job), the one that would provide security (the first card drawn).

Finally I'm looking at that **Emperor reversed**, and I'm realizing that Joe has probably been browbeaten into some kind of submission and he doesn't have what it takes to fight back. Fathers tend to be hard for guys to deal with, at least until they enter their thirties. The kid wants to please the man, whether he deserves respect and pleasing or not.

I tell Joe all of this. He nods.

I now ask him the first question: "Are you working?"

"No."

"It looks to me like you're not even looking. Are you okay?"

Joe nods. "Right. I'm not looking." He pauses, "What do you mean 'okay'?"

"Well, this depression here," I say as I point to the Star. "Are you seeing a doctor about it?"

"No," Joe says.

And it strikes me all of a sudden it's as if this guy has just collapsed into a life he has no sense he can control and, worse, he has no awareness of the fact that something is just plain wrong here.

So now I need to know: "But how are you going to pay your bills if you don't have a job?"

"I don't know exactly," he says. "Maybe something will come along." He pauses, gestures at the cards on the table. "Isn't it there?"

Oh, no. I get it. This is a young guy who has come looking for magic. Not the Merlin kind of magic, but the kind of magical thinking psychology talks about: Joe simply needs to believe that the answers he seeks are outside himself, that he himself has no responsibility to make decisions, and that I am to be the answer today.

This is a dangerous road for both of us. I can't ethically tell him fairy tales, and Joe shouldn't even be asking for them. Just asking is pointing to a dark and self-destructive place.

So now I have to put another card on that reversed Emperor. Magical thinking doesn't come out of nowhere, I know. It's an aspect of addiction. **The Devil** falls.

"Joe, is your father an alcoholic?" This isn't such a shot in the dark. Depression and sugar issues / alcoholism aren't that far apart, I've learned.

"Yes," he says. And since I've also learned that addiction is genetic and the predisposition is inherited, I understand that maybe Joe is being physically and chemically affected by his own system and some kind of sugar thing.

Worse, I then add a card to the Emperor and the Devil and it's the **Knight of Swords reversed** (destructiveness). I add another card to elaborate on this, and it's the **Five of Swords reversed** (anger). Anger and destructiveness falling on top of a card that all by itself talks about a domineering and bullying authority figure? Now I know that what I'm seeing is an abused child in an environment where rage was the rule and out-of-the-blue attacks were no doubt common. (Some doctors compare this kind of childhood with soldiers' experience in wartime. The soldiers who come back with PTSD.)

"Joe, did your dad get drunk and abuse you physically?"

"Me and my brother both. All the time." He says it too matter-of-factly. Damn it, he should be angry ...

And so I think, no wonder the poor guy has no dreams. No wonder he isn't trying. In a very real sense, I realize that Joe is emotionally broken, on top of the depression. This is just not great. He needs real professional help. And that ain't me.

"Joe, I know why you think you came here today, but this is really, really more important. It's possible you have post-traumatic stress disorder on top of the depression. At the very least, you were an abused kid."

Joe nods.

But now, for the first time since he walked in thirty minutes ago, he seems to generate some physical and emotional energy. "Wait, you mean what I have might have a name? PTSD?"

"And depression."

"Well, that's something people can fix, right?"

"As a rule, I think yes."

Joe sits up. "My father's always telling me I'm dumb and incompetent and that anything I dream of I could never get to anyway. So I finally figured, why try?" He paused. "You mean I could actually make something of my life?"

I draw a couple of cards. The **King of Pentacles** (a solid working man, reliable) and the **Ten of Cups** (a lovely marriage).

I say, "Not only can you make something of your life. If you want to, Joe, you can even make it spectacular. It's right here." If the cards had been bad, I would have said nothing. *People in need of healing need to believe they can be healed.*

Also, I didn't want to spoil Joe's eureka moment by asking about his mother, who I figure did nothing to protect her children from their father and who, therefore, was the worse problem. Children look to their moms for protection, and they get a real bad self-image if the mother doesn't do that protecting.

Joe has become pensive now. But it seems he's also been acquiring some energy, some passion, some *juice* in the last couple of minutes.

I ask now, both curious and wanting to change the subject and relieve the pressure for a sec, "So who sent you to me?"

"My friend," Joe responded. "She said you could help me."

I laughed, like we were suddenly conspirators, which is exactly how I felt. "So really you came here to get help."

Joe laughed, sheepish. "Yeah, I guess I did."

"Well," I told him, "that's about the best thing you could *ever* know. I mean, if a person doesn't have the desire to get help, that person can never get well. See? Just *wanting* it is the whole enchilada, as far as I'm concerned."

And this guy smiles now for maybe the first time in a while. For the first time ever? All of a sudden, somebody is giving his "thing" a name and telling him it can be dealt with? And so, for the first time he can remember, he has *hope*?

See, if I never do another thing for Joe, this ability to convey hope to him will have been everything.

I now have to warn him, though, that addiction runs in families. So he has to be very careful of alcohol and drugs and high-sugar foods. I tell him it would be way too easy for him to slip down into the dark world where his father lives.

Joe nods. "I read some stuff about that." So he's known ...

"So promise me you'll be careful? *All* your life?"

Joe promises.

"And promise me you will see a psychotherapist this week, no delays, so you can get started on the path to your dreams and your plans and your joy."

Joe promises.

"Do you know somebody you can call for an appointment?"

Joe shrugs. No.

So I give him the name and number of a therapist I totally respect and trust. He folds the paper and puts it quite carefully into his shirt pocket. Just from this I can tell he's going to at least try to follow through.

"And get some books and DVDs by John Bradshaw. He works a lot with grown-up kids from addictive, domestic-violent homes. I think he can help you too. Just get the things at the library."

"I promise."

This is at the thirty-minute mark. The reading is over.

And with this last promise, Joe leaves my office with kind of a spring in his step that wasn't there before, with his head held higher than before.

Joe has come back to life.

After this, I never saw the guy again. But a couple years later, the friend who'd sent him came to me and told me that Joe always said he owed me his life. I said, "No way. *He* did it. Whatever he's accomplished, it's all a credit to him."

She said, "He went to the therapist you recommended, and he started working hard to find a job. And he did it. It wasn't a great job at first, but it was paying the bills, and he started to be proud of himself. Finally." She paused. "He said to tell you thanks."

And this is exactly the kind of story that makes me cry.

Allie's Getting Married!

Love is a tricky thing. Sometimes we're so desperate to have it in our lives that we mistake neediness or dependence for love. I was married for seven years to a guy who didn't know how to love but sure knew how to use the word. Finally, when we were splitting up, I asked him about it, and his answer told me that from the start we'd been operating with two totally different definitions of that big, huge word "love."

✳ ✳ ✳

Well, Allie is head over heels in love. She comes into my office and plops down on the chair across from me. A new client. Pretty, sparkling brown eyes, auburn hair shiny as heck, with a really nice diamond glittering on the ring finger of her left hand. (Ordinarily, I don't want to see this. I don't want to know anything about the client. But they show up and then I have to work to ignore what's in front of my face.)

"So, hi, Allie. How are you doing?"

She's a girl in maybe her mid-twenties. Savvy. I figure she'd be fun to be with at parties.

"Okay," she says.

Then I make my usual speech because I need to get all my information from the cards, at least at the start. "Now, don't tell me anything about your life yet, okay? Just give me seven cards, one at a time, from this pile on the table."

Allie draws seven cards kind of fast, hands them to me, and sits back. Confident.

The first card she's given me, the *issue*, is the **Ten of Cups reversed** (a bad marriage).

The seventh card, the *outcome*, is **Justice** (some kind of legal action relating to marriage: usually that's divorce).

Ouch. I'm looking at this and I'm looking at her diamond, and I'm hoping she's *already* been divorced.

I say nothing for now. I need the other cards to fill out the picture.

I lay them down: the **King of Rods/Wands reversed** (a man who doesn't want to commit; *not* to be confused with a man who doesn't want to marry ... this guy may just not be faithful); the **Empress reversed** (a woman not emotionally mature enough to be a wife); the **Page of Pentacles reversed** (somebody should be studying something but doesn't want to have to do it); the **King of Pentacles** (a dependable, reliable provider); and the **Two of Cups reversed** (it isn't actually love that's being shared, if this card refers to Allie and her fiancé).

I am now praying hard that this sweet girl isn't here to ask about her forthcoming marriage. But not all prayers get answered. I'll soon learn that's exactly why she's here.

First, of course, I have to talk. And I can't censor myself. This girl has a right to know what I see. It's one of those times when I hope I'm wrong.

I *say* so.

"Allie, I hope I'm wrong, but I'm looking at a marriage where there's no real love, the husband is not committed to the vows, the wife isn't emotionally ready to be a wife, somebody should be in school but doesn't want to be, and the person probably thinks her man will be taking care of her instead." I pause. "Does any of this ring a bell?"

"No." She shrugs.

"It doesn't describe your parents?" I'm hoping. Sometimes the parents show up first, if the daughter or son hasn't really gotten away from their influence yet.

"Not at all," she kind of exclaims. "They've been so happy together for so long, it's what gives me hope about my own marriage." She extends her left hand. "See?"

"Yes, I saw."

Then I think, well, it *is* possible: "So have you been married before?"

"No. This is my first—and only—time."

I smile to be encouraging. But my heart is sinking.

"So maybe you have a sister or brother?"

"Nope. Only child." And now she starts to wonder: "Why are you asking me all of this stuff?"

"How old are you? Mid-twenties?"

"Twenty-five," she announces proudly.

And so now I know: I have seen it, astrologers talk about it, and even Dr. Daniel Goleman, a psychiatrist, wrote in the *New York Times* a while ago that adolescence doesn't end until we're in our early thirties. (This would be in line with the Saturn return in astrology and the notion that the human body isn't even completely formed until that time.)

Which means to me, a tarot reader with a lot of experience under her belt, that almost nobody aged twenty-five is ready for marriage, at least not as a life-long possibility. Not in this day and age. Variety is just too easy to find.

She adds, proudly, "We've been in true love for six years."

Oh my. So sweet and innocent. Which means she met this young man in her late teens. Talk about not being mature enough for a step like marriage.

But I have to do what I do. It's not an option.

"Allie, if nobody around you fits that marriage scenario, then it has to be you. I hope I'm totally wrong, but..."

The girl jumps up now, rattling the table. "Oh, you are *so* wrong. I can't believe you would say this stuff. My friend said you're good. What a crock."

"I didn't choose the cards, Allie."

"Well, then you just don't know what you're doing, and I'm leaving, and I'm not paying you." The session has lasted all of maybe ten minutes.

I don't argue. I let her go. I will let her be in her bliss until everything hits the fan.

I never see her again.

But let me say this about such a scenario: This girl, instead of delighting in her engagement every minute of every day, had come to *me* for...for *what*? Reassurance? For encouragement that she wasn't making a mistake? Seeking happy tidings about the forthcoming nuptials?

I believed then, and I still do, that as with others I've worked with, something deep in Allie just wasn't a hundred percent sure she was doing the right thing. And *that's* the real reason why she came to me. And as with the magical thinking that was happening here, she had no interest in anything but good news. So in her mind, what I was saying just couldn't be.

* * *

A year or so later, a client I'd worked with a few times came back.

"You remember a girl named Allie? She came to see you in January, and you said her marriage wasn't going to work out?"

"Yes, I remember." The truth was I'd wondered about it often ever since.

"Well, they got married, and like you said, it lasted six months." The friend paused. "She really should've listened to you."

But I know, from my own experience in life and with clients, that if we don't make mistakes, then we don't grow, and if we don't grow, then where are we?

So Allie made a mistake. In the grand scheme of things, not the biggest possible one.

Some people even call it a "starter marriage" these days, kind of like training wheels on a two-wheeler. You do it, you do it wrong, you figure out what you did wrong, and with luck you never do it again.

See, this is really important for a reader to know: Many females are just plain obsessed with getting married, for many different reasons. But obsession has nothing to do with informed choice or even desire. It has more to do with a kind of desperation. *Webster's Dictionary* defines *obsession* as "a persistent disturbing preoccupation with an often unreasonable idea or feeling." For sure, this kind of thing is nothing to base a wedding on, never mind a lifetime. And the reader can spot it because the obsessed person is a hundred percent involved in the obsession and will allow nothing to get in the way of that. You're doing a reading and the *client keeps coming back* to the same questions: Where is he? When is he coming?

Just tell these people what you see and hope for the best for them.

And tell them you hope you're wrong.

And mean it.

CHAPTER 10

TAROT AS A LANGUAGE

This chapter deals with the nuts and bolts of my approach to tarot as a language (like French or Spanish) and the way you can see for yourself how this works. I think the following little exercise will help you understand what I was getting at earlier.

Take four small pieces of paper. On the first, write *house*. On the second, write *yellow*. On the third, write *ranch-style*. On the fourth, write *intersection*.

Now line these papers up, upside down, in a horizontal row on the table.

Now turn over the first paper and read *aloud,* "House."

Now turn over the second and read, "Yellow house."

Now turn over the third and read, "Yellow ranch house."

Now turn over the fourth and read, "Yellow ranch house [at an] intersection."

From now on in this chapter, take the cards I'm talking about, place them where I say, and speak aloud what I write.

Take your cards and remove the Seven of Cups, the Five of Pentacles reversed, the Three of Pentacles, and the Ace of Cups. Line these up on the table from left to right.

If you turn these cards over one at a time, you can read: *Dreaming of/finding a job/that is a high-level job/that I will love.* See? It's as clear as day! And there's no guessing.

But if you're looking at only one card, the Seven of Cups (*dreaming*), how are you going to have an accurate idea of what the dream is? The answer is you're not. And so you're going to try to guess, and you're going to call that "psychic" work. Well, I call it "guesswork," and I know it happens all the time, because too many readers out there tend to be vague. Or downright wrong. And that's why.

But by *continuing to add* cards beside a card until you have a complete thought, you'll be right on the money in terms of what you can tell your client. My clients say they've never seen anyone else do this. As I've said, it just kind of came to me one day, like pretty much everything else I've discovered about tarot. So far, anyway.

Sometimes I start with the basic seven cards, and by the time I'm done, I have as many as thirty or forty cards on the table, because I needed them all to give me the whole story in detail. Also, when the reading starts, I try to speak for a while without interruption. The client gives me the first seven cards, and I just keep taking more cards and talking from that point on.

When you finally let your client ask a question, you should already have a good general idea of his or her life and situation. So now you have a context for the details that come next. Not to mention that if you get good at this, you can sometimes answer every question at the very beginning before anything has even been asked. After that it's all about detail and depth, elaboration and clarification. But the basics you've probably already touched on. Nailed.

So now, one thing about that first card:

Card 1 is the issue at hand. For the purposes of this exercise, let's say our client is asking about her job.

Card 1, the issue, is the Four of Rods/Wands. What this means is that she's looking at the job *from that point of view.* The client sees it as a nice, collegial environment with nice coworkers. So the issue is this: she sees it as a "good" job really just because of the people there.

Card 7, the outcome, is the Six of Swords reversed. So now you know that the nice environment (the Four of Rods/Wands: the way she's looking at the job) is leading her to choose to stay in a lousy situation (the Six of Swords reversed).

Card 2 is the King of Rods/Wands reversed: maybe she has a bad manager or disloyal manager, or her husband is not committed to her or supporting her somehow when it comes to her job.

Card 3 is the Seven of Swords: there's politics in the workplace, deception; she's somehow being ripped off at the job.

Card 4 is the Page of Pentacles: she needs to study something if she's going to be able to make a good change.

Card 5 is the Ace of Cups reversed: there is no gratification or satisfaction for her in this job.

Card 6 is the Ten of Rods/Wands reversed: on top of everything else, she's burned out.

Now you can say this aloud: *Because your coworkers are nice, you're staying at a lousy job that doesn't pay and isn't satisfying; you have a disloyal boss; and you're burned out.*

At this point, you need to think like a logical person. If something were going to change, what would it be? If you, the reader, were in this situation, what would *you* do?

Well, one of the first seven cards your client chose in this case is about something she *can* do while staying at her job.

The one card that tells you she can take action? The Page of Pentacles (the student; study).

So you lay a card beside this and you get the Eight of Pentacles (a challenging job with a learning curve that pays okay).

Then, just out of "curiosity," you add a card to the Four of Rods/Wands and it is the Tower (something's going to happen to shake up that nice working atmosphere).

So then you add a card to the Ace of Cups and it turns out to be the Three of Swords. For this client, not having a gratifying job is the pits, if not downright painful, regardless of how nice the colleagues are.

By the time you finish answering the job question, you can have progressed the current situation into the future by adding cards to each basic card and going where they take you.

And so you can tell your client the situation is going to change around her (the Tower), but if she studies (the Page of Pentacles), she can move on to something better, something that's challenging and pays well (the Eight of Pentacles).

Listen, it takes a lot of practice to do this stuff, but it can be done. Once you start actually doing it, you'll just get it. It makes so much sense. I can't picture *house*, but I *can* picture a yellow ranch house at an intersection.

Also, I am a natural-born reporter. In my head, as I'm reading, I'm always asking *why?* and *what?* This is what I mean by "curiosity." You need to *want* to get all the details so you can tell the most complete story you can. (It's a yellow ranch house, not a blue split-level. It matters.)

Finally, as I said before, always practice aloud. There's something about speaking what you see that either reinforces your logic or tells you, wait, this doesn't sound right. Speaking always forces us to put our thoughts into coherent communication. So begin now, and from now on, always practice aloud.

One Small Point That's Kind of Big When It Comes to Translation

Translating Chinese into English is a challenge. In that language, there's no word for "the" or "a." But in English, it's all about *connectives*. This is a big word for usually small things we use every day, all day long, without even thinking about it.

In reading tarot cards the way we read sentences, we can do the same thing just as easily.

Here's what I mean:

At the beginning of this chapter, I asked you to write four words on pieces of paper.

The result was *yellow ranch house [at an] intersection*.

No, you didn't write "at an" on a piece of paper. But what else could the four words mean? A yellow ranch intersection house? No. So if you think about it, it has to be a house at an intersection *if it's going to make any sense*.

In a reading, for example, sometimes you'll have someone putting out a résumé (the Seven of Rods/Wands) sitting next to no money (the Six of Pentacles reversed). Once you know the meanings of the cards, you'll simply say,

"Putting out a résumé *because* there's no money." You won't even think twice. The logic of the sentence will simply happen.

Would you have a woman in love leave a man in love? No. So if she's going to do this, there has to be a *reason*. There has to be a *because*.

It's the same with *next to, about, from, but, and,* and whatever other connective comes to mind as you're doing a reading and need it to make sense.

A man has a job *but* he has a house? Well, that makes no sense, right? So it must be: A man has a job *and* he has a house.

In my system of understanding tarot as a language, this is the only thing you'll ever have to add, really, to make sense: the connectives. But again, I have a student who suddenly just started doing it: making sense as she connected the cards. It just started happening.

And since the cards will always make sense, it will keep becoming easier to know the meaning of a card. A woman is happy because she's in a bad marriage? No way. So look around at the cards on the table and see if you can find the card(s) that can tell you *why* she's happy.

To make sure you have a good grasp of what's going on here, in chapter 20 I give you a list of clauses, phrases, and sentences in English. Your job is to "translate" the English into tarot cards. To do this, you won't be reading cards. But you'll be *understanding* them.

I invented this exercise, and I think it's a really important part of your training. My students love it. They love the challenge of expressing ideas in pictures, even though most of them don't know most of the card meanings yet when I start asking them to do this. They use the book, they find the right cards, and they learn.

And once you've exhausted the list in chapter 20, take any sentences or logical strings of words and try to translate them into cards.

For the purposes of this exercise, you might say that the sections on definitions of the cards in this book are a kind of tarot-to-English dictionary.

Language Barriers

I've learned about this issue the hard way. The most difficult thing for me to do as a reader is to try to work with somebody whose grasp of English is not too good. I have to try hard sometimes to tell people what I'm seeing when they don't have a vocabulary. I can speak in simple terms to people without much education and we may have successful sessions. But even simple words and terms can elude somebody for whom English is a second or even third language. This makes it impossible for me to convey nuances, big ideas. It's utterly frustrating for both me and the client. So now, when I believe I'm hearing a really thick accent on the phone when an appointment is being made, I ask the person how good his or her command of English is. I mean, I don't want to take money from somebody I know in my heart I'm not really going to be able to help.

So all I can say here is that if you're confronted with this situation, just do the best you can to be clear and make yourself understood.

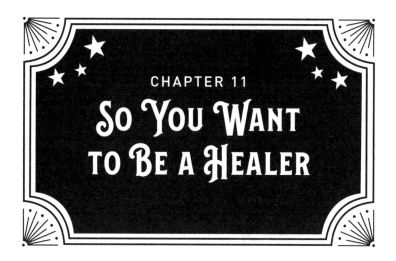

CHAPTER 11

So You Want to Be a Healer

When I wrote this book, it was designed for people who dream of and desire to work in some way as a healer. No, I'm not a healer, but I do consider myself part of a healing modality, kind of a link in a healing chain. This chapter deals with this and my thinking about how psychics and mystics can work successfully in the world of healing. (Please see chapters 13 and 14, where I talk about the card combinations that relate to health and health issues.)

You can't imagine how gratifying it is for me to see how many people these days dream of helping others. Most of my students fall into this category. A great many of my clients do too.

But I've also noticed there are an awful lot of false impressions out there about this thing people are calling "healing."

See, I just can't imagine it's possible for most people to spend a weekend learning something like reiki, for example, and then be qualified to go out and fix the world. And I also doubt that two days of hypnotism training is going to prepare most people to deal with all the emotional and psychological issues that true hypnosis can raise.

And for sure you cannot learn to work with tarot in a day.

So what I think is happening here is that most folks with really good intentions are getting sucked into the idea that they can work miracles without putting in any effort. *And* get paid for it.

Well, face it, please! There's a lot of walking to do before any of us can run. And before that we have to crawl for a while. And I don't care what we're talking about here. I mean, would you live in a house built by a guy who's never picked up a hammer? Would you turn on a toaster if the electrician hasn't been licensed? Would you leave your baby with somebody who's never cared for an infant? Of course not! (Well, I hope not.)

See, there's no difference when working with oracles and nontraditional healing methods. Everything great takes time. But for the dreamer with the talent *and* the willingness to put in the time to learn to do things right, there are no limits.

My Definition of Healing

Over the years I've developed a definition of healing that works for me and my clients. I call what I do "therapeutic," because my goal is to give my clients the tools they need to heal themselves.

This is especially true of emotional, psychological and psychiatric issues.

Psychology

Over the years, more than a few people have told me that *I'm* their "therapy." NOT! I just can't discourage that thinking fast enough.

Yes, as a reader I may be able to see clearly what's going on and, with any luck at all, *why* it's going on. But just because I say the thing out loud doesn't mean it's gone. I mean, I have a degree in English, not psychology!

And I've also noticed that the people who most want to see me as a therapist are the very same people who need professional help the most. But they're afraid of the work—and the pain—that therapy can involve.

To deal with this, I try to have on hand the names and numbers of some good therapists so I can refer my clients for real healing help. (I totally respect and appreciate medium Jeffrey Wands in this regard, because at the end of his book *Another Door Opens*, he names the therapists to whom *he* refers people when he knows his work isn't enough.)

So I consider it my job as a "healer" to give my clients the information they need to go out and make themselves whole. See, when you work from compassion, this is part of the role. Out of compassion, I'm doing nothing more than pointing people in the right direction.

Even Good Things Have Limits

I also refuse to read people too often, as I've said. I refuse to become a crutch in the life of a client. What good am I doing a person if he or she can't get up in the morning and make even one decision without consulting me? As I wrote earlier, the only decent thing to do is not be that available.

I once had a client named Nancy who was obsessed with the idea that her boyfriend was seeing somebody else. She was calling me almost every day about this. But I had already seen and explained everything she needed to know and do the *first* time she came to me. (No, see, he didn't have anybody else. But Nancy's fears were out of control. So the first time we met, I suggested she talk to a professional about what was really going on in her: an obsession.)

She stopped calling when I refused once and for all to read for her for at least three months.

And what did she do next? She went out and found one of those storefront "psychics" we see everywhere (those "spiritual advisers"). That person, who of course had no psychic ability at all, didn't have any pesky little ethical stumbling blocks and was more than willing to scare Nancy silly about her boyfriend on a daily basis.

This woman ending up hurting Nancy. A lot. She encouraged her obsession, her fears, her jealousy, the sleeplessness. And she took all her money.

Eventually Nancy came back to me, told me the story, and was utterly ashamed for being "so stupid." (Which, of course, she wasn't. She was simply not well.)

As for me, I wanted to just go and nail that "psychic" who'd nearly destroyed what was left of my sweet client's heart and psyche.

Of course I didn't. But, hey, I was totally ticked off, disgusted.

And by the way, not all my clients are success stories. They get the truth from me and they get referrals, but they don't all go home and pick up the phone to do what they need to do to get well. They all have my prayers, always.

So, What Is "Spiritual"?

My belief is that psychic work is not—repeat, *not*—"spiritual." In the same way that animals seem to know beforehand that a natural disaster is about to strike, I believe we humans are blessed with psychic ability, a *biological* function, as a defense mechanism to keep us safe in what can be a very dangerous world.

For example, if I see any combination of the Five of Swords reversed, the Seven of Swords, the Knight of Swords reversed, and Justice reversed, I warn my client to be careful of being robbed, mugged, attacked. I see what can happen if the client becomes careless, and I warn the person so it can be prevented.

Animals have built-in scent and eyesight detectors and some kind of ability to "know" there's danger around the next corner. I think we have the very same ability; we just aren't always aware of it.

The Art of Medicine

At some point in my self-education on oracles, I read that Hippocrates required new physicians to know astrology so they could tell which part of a person's body was most predisposed to fail. This was in long-ago Greece. Today we have X-rays and blood tests, MRIs and CAT scans. But it doesn't mean that astrology no longer works as a diagnostic tool.

And I've learned that tarot can work the same way.

Learning to identify health issues with tarot is like learning symptoms in medical school. It takes time and study and practice to use cards to pinpoint medical problems, the same way it takes time and study and practice to know what a blood test result means. It takes information about life. And it takes information about diseases and how we get them. But like the hard-working medical student, if you care enough, if you want it bad enough, you'll do what it takes to get there.

When I started finding health information in cards, I wasn't out there looking for it. It started with the Irish girl with the brain tumor (from chapter 5), and after a while it was like the floodgates opened. People came to me with health problems, and a lot of the time I was able to see what was going on.

Still, one client, Chris, got really mad at me. She came for a reading about her husband, but somewhere in the middle of it I saw a "thyroid problem" for her. Apparently, I told Chris on that point that everything would be "fine."

Well, a few months later her "thyroid problem" turned out to be cancer, and she went through six months of hell and a huge surgery.

But she did end up "fine." So why was she mad? Because I hadn't seen all that stuff between her diagnosis and her cure.

What could I say? All I'd seen was a very nice ending to a lousy story. But she was so disgusted and mad at me that she never came back!

Now, do I have any medical training? No. Do I have in-depth knowledge of anatomy and how the body works? No. But I *do* have life experience.

Here's an example. One day I was reading a guy, and all of a sudden, for the first time, I noticed that one of the people on one of my cards had a blue hand. Mind you, I'd been using this pack for fifteen years at that point. But I guess I'd never noticed the hand before because I'd never *needed* to.

Anyway, I see this blue hand, and I suddenly remember a story about my brother-in-law. Twenty years earlier, he'd been diagnosed with Raynaud's disease, a circulation problem that makes the fingers blue when it's cold. So I asked my client if he had a circulation problem.

"Yes," he said.

I asked, "Do you smoke?" (My brother-in-law smoked like a chimney.)

"Yes," he said.

So I told my client what my brother-in-law's doctor had told him, "Quit smoking or else!" I'm glad my client decided then and there to clean up his act. I don't know if it helped his hands. For sure it helped his lungs.

Likewise, the former mayor of New York City, Ed Koch, had a series of minor strokes a few years back. They were called TIAs (transient ischemic attacks). Sure enough, TIAs have come up a few times in readings since I learned what they are from the *New York Daily News*.

At this point I have a feeling that all we have to do is live long enough and things will start to go wrong with our bodies, and so we'll learn physiology the hard way. (Same thing with cars. They dime you to death is what some mechanics say about the old ones.) Anyway, you'll probably end up learning a lot about medicine just trying to get yourself fixed.

Meanwhile, the longer you're on this earth, the more people you'll meet, the more people you'll read about, the more TV you'll watch (yes, like *House!*), and the more you'll learn, just by osmosis. Michael J. Fox loses control of his hands because of Parkinson's disease. Christopher Reeve had breathing problems due to a spinal cord injury. Annette Funicello ended up in a wheelchair due to multiple sclerosis.

Then there is everything my clients have taught me through their readings. As I wrote earlier, through readings I learned of the relationship between breast cancer and repressed anger, the side effects of some medications, everything I know about addiction, and so much more.

Finally, good newspaper advice columnists, like the late Abigail Van Buren (*Dear Abby*), always consulted doctors when readers wrote letters about medical problems. And I always read the columns. From these columns you can learn so much about people and love, people and fears, people and pain, people and problems.

And don't make it harder than it is. You don't have to actually name a disease or disorder. All you have to do is see the symptoms and describe them. Your client and his or her physician can do the rest. This is not practicing medicine, by the way. I always end a reading like this by telling the client to consult a doctor. And I never say anybody *should* do this or that. I have no right. And when it comes to medicine, it's usually not legal to do that. So I simply offer what I think is an apt diagnosis when I see it.

Bottom line, if you want to help people in any way, you can't live and work in a vacuum. You have to know things about things. You have to understand that your clients come to you from different backgrounds and with different lifestyles and with many different kinds of issues. You have to read the news every day and know what's going on in the world. It's like writing fiction: the more you know, the more you can draw on and the more you can flesh out, and the stronger the writing will be.

And for you beginners out there, it *can* happen early on that you'll see something medical or deeply psychological and you'll tell your client about it. And this will be a good thing. But, more likely, it won't happen at all until you're not a beginner anymore.

In the end, we can all help only the people we are meant to help.

Have faith in that.

CHAPTER 12

Figuring Out What's Wrong

In this chapter I talk about the nuts and bolts of reading tarot cards to identify health issues.

The Traditional Way

Before I start talking about using tarot to identify health issues, it might help to think for a minute about what a doctor does when somebody comes in with a problem. First the doctor asks questions like: Where does it hurt? How long has it been like that? Have you been running a fever? Can you keep food down? Any digestive problems? Do you feel faint? Any history of a problem in your family?

Then a physical exam is done and tests are ordered: white blood cell count (to check for infection), red blood cell count, occult blood in stool, X-rays, scans, sonograms. The doctor has been trained to know the magic number for white and red blood cells, what it can mean if there's blood in the stool, and so forth. To the doctor, a little too much of this or that is a marker for a specific illness.

So, at last, the doctor puts together what you've told him with what he's found in the exam and the results of the tests, and he is able (with luck) to give your problem a name and a fix.

The Tarot Way

Using tarot to do this is much the same, except that with the tarot we may be able to see the answers without even asking the questions. A good reader may be able to see what the lab tests and X-rays and exam can lead to. And a good reader can put all of this together with what he or she knows about life, from experience, and come up with a pretty good description of a medical problem.

Do you need to know the word "colitis" to tell somebody about a problem with the digestive system? No. You don't need to know the name of a thing to see it. You don't have to know about cardiology to warn about heart disease or high blood pressure or high cholesterol.

All of this is predicated, of course, on the idea that the reader has the "doctor muscle."

But many do. It's these people who'll tend to attract the patient-clients.

Card Smart

What you *do* have to know, though, is which cards relate to which parts of the body as a rule, and which cards—usually the Major Arcana—describe the various diseases and problems. (See the next chapter for details.)

For example, if you know that Strength reversed is infection and the Devil means chronic, then these two cards together can mean chronic infection. And if you know that the Knight of Cups reversed is seduction and the Seven of Swords is guilt or deception, then you can put all of this together. Someone seductive lies to you (or omits the truth) and that person has a chronic infection. This is how HIV appears for me in a reading. And when I see it, I warn my client to be careful. No unprotected sex and no sex with strangers, because somebody around you may not be telling you the truth about his or her health picture.

In the next chapter we're going to look at which cards—and which *combinations of cards*—can indicate to me specific medical problems. These you too can learn, memorize, and, with luck, use effectively.

As time goes on, you can add your own to the list.

Suppose your Aunt Harriet had diabetes and lost her foot to gangrene, and you remember your mother saying that your aunt's foot turned black before she lost it. And suppose now you're reading for someone and you see a black foot (or think you do). Right off, your Aunt Harriet is going to come to mind, and you'll be jumping to diabetes before you know it. I myself associate diabetes with injections, so I see a Sword reversed and Temperance reversed (imbalance) and I read it correctly as diabetes.

The point here is that a tarot reader's own life experience is crucial. Always. Whatever *you* associate with certain things will trigger thoughts you might otherwise never have had! So we both get to the right disease by two different roads. Sort of like the acupuncturist who sticks needles in somebody to relieve pain and the doctor who prescribes aspirin for that pain. Both are right, and maybe one is no better than the other, but they both sure are different approaches!

Bottom line here: You can learn from me, but you don't have to be limited by what I tell you. The people who need *you* in particular will find *you* in particular because you'll be somebody who knows what they need to hear. Trust me on this.

And one final, very important point I have to make again: I am not a doctor. I do not practice medicine. What I do is try to give people information they can use to pinpoint and resolve the problems their bodies and minds are having. Before somebody with a problem leaves my table, I always encourage the person to seek professional help. This I cannot repeat enough: *Always* send potentially sick clients to doctors.

CHAPTER 13

Health and the Major Arcana

In this chapter I explain how the Major Arcana cards appear in readings to convey the idea of health issues and how some of these cards can relate to others.

The Cards When They Stand Alone

When you see several of certain Major cards together on the table, including the Devil, Temperance reversed, the Magician (upright or reversed), and Strength reversed, you should think you might be looking at some kind of illness. More than one of these can be pointing to health as the subject matter of a spread. It's the very presence of more than one of these cards that tells me I'm probably dealing with health and not some other subject.

So, just like a doctor who wants to know if there's a fever, how long you've had it, and if there's a rash—the various medical "markers" of something specific—the reader has to be on the lookout for the presence of two or more health-related cards.

See, a fever all by itself is not necessarily a terrible thing, and so something like Temperance reversed is not necessarily a terrible thing. But a fever with a bunch of other stuff you've had for two weeks—suddenly that doesn't look so good, right? In the same way, if you see Temperance reversed with *other* health cards, you can be pretty sure you're looking at a larger health problem. Trust me.

And in all of this, when you see a *behavior* issue, always look for *why*.

The Devil

This card is a huge indicator (marker). Upright, it means chronic, malignant, critical, very bad.

So the presence of the Devil in a reading automatically makes something not so minor anymore. Almost every time the Devil shows up, the reader needs to look carefully at what else is around or added to it. For example, the Devil and the Ten of Rods/Wands (exhaustion) can mean chronic fatigue. The Devil and the Two of Rods/Wands reversed (confusion) can mean Alzheimer's disease.

Basically, you don't want to see the Devil ever, unless it's about great sex (when it can make a rare appearance).

But you *do* want to see the Devil *reversed*, because this means something bad being cured or healed or overcome or absent.

This is especially true when you also see the Magician with the Devil: upright, this is a person who heals. So the presence of the Magician upright means that the client is in good hands, the doctor is competent, the problem is curable. Combined with the Devil reversed, it's even better news. (Of course, you may not see all of that bad stuff between the diagnosis and the cure, and your client may get mad at you, but still…)

This curing includes alcoholism, by the way. The Devil plus Temperance reversed plus the Magician equals recovery. In the case of addiction, it is the person in recovery who is symbolized by all three cards. You know, sometimes this one little piece of information can be enough to encourage an addict to try to overcome an addiction, simply because you see that he or she can.

By the way, I include alcoholism in the addiction category, along with obesity, degenerate gambling, compulsive spending, and workaholism. All of these things anesthetize us so we can't feel pain—but then we can't feel joy or love either. What does this mean for those of us who love the addict? Nothing good.

The Magician

The Magician upright describes a successful healer, a curable problem. But if this card shows up reversed, it means the doctor is not successful or the doctor may not be competent. In this case, if illness is involved, I suggest the client consider getting a second opinion. (This was the case when Molly had both a doctor and an undiagnosed tumor.)

The Magician reversed can also be an incurable condition.

Temperance

Temperance is a sign of health, usually holistic health. It can be a sign of a good diet, of the right amount of food and drink in the diet. If it's reversed, though, my mind goes to a hormone imbalance, an insulin problem, not enough water in the diet, too much salt, or too much sugar.

And I can tell the difference between a dietary problem and an illness, because when it's a diet problem, I also tend to see the Four of Cups (temptation) and/or the Seven of Swords (guilt) and maybe the Lovers (a lifestyle *choice*).

If the Devil doesn't show up at all, the situation is probably not at the critical stage. So at this point you might think that your client is eating all wrong as a way of dealing with problems and that he or she just has to find another way to handle them. If your client needs to find another way to deal with loneliness besides eating a whole cake, well, there's running. There's swimming (no impact). There's jogging, spinning, and yoga. There's even eating something else, like salad or air-popped corn. There's also sweating to the oldies and being proud of yourself, instead of feeling guilty every time you turn around.

I usually mention all of these options when my client confirms there's an eating problem. (And by the way, this stuff can be detected over the phone, sight unseen.)

Temperance upright or reversed can also indicate medications, the pulmonary system (lungs), fluid-related issues (excluding blood), and hormone issues.

In the case of both Temperance reversed and the Devil, there can be an addiction to prescription drugs, and not just illegal ones. In this case, along with the drug cards I usually see the "crutch" cards: the Four of Pentacles and/or the Knight of Pentacles reversed.

Now, if drugs (Temperance) show up with the Seven of Swords (guilt) and Justice (the law), I know the substance in question might be controlled or illegal. Which means we're probably not talking about alcohol, which is legal everywhere at a certain age.

And Temperance reversed can also indicate a virus, even just a cold. (Again, if the Devil also shows up, that virus could be a killer.)

So if you were to see, for example, Temperance reversed, the Four of Cups, the Seven of Swords, *and* the Devil, it may mean your client has graduated from overeating to a serious food disorder. (Anorexia and bulimia can also be symbolized in part by Temperance reversed.)

And serious food disorders are self-destructive: they require both medical *and* psychological intervention. Somebody is hurting himself or herself in a cycle of pain and self-punishment. This is a very vicious and painful cycle.

Strength

Strength is a nice card to see when you're dealing with a health question. Basically, it tells you the client is strong enough to handle the issue. Essentially strong, essentially healthy. It means your client can fight off a disease more easily than frail old Aunt Edna, whose resistance may have been compromised by age.

Strength reversed, though, can mean infection. It can mean no resistance, no immune-system strength. Strength reversed can mean that someone is basically not strong. When I see this card, I suggest a checkup and a better diet, just in case.

And when it comes to mind over matter, Strength can mean a sick person will be well because that's where their head is at: determined. Lance Armstrong comes to mind here. He was given six weeks to live because a cancer that had pervaded his body had invaded his brain. I can hear him now: no way! And that was years ago.

Justice

Justice in a health spread, and it's *not* about illegal drugs? Sure! As I said earlier, a major symbol in this card is the scales, and I've discovered that this card can show up reversed to tell me somebody's weight is not what it should be. (It's a scale issue.) Or maybe the client is having problems with balance. Add the

Devil and you can have chronic imbalance, vertigo (loss of the sense of balance), or chronic weight issues. Add Temperance reversed and you can have a chronic hormonal imbalance, maybe a middle ear infection.

The Tower

Upright, the Tower is shaking up your life. It can also be a sudden neurological problem, a stroke. With the Two of Wands reversed (confusion), it can be a sudden incident involving the brain that causes confusion or an inability to think.

With the Knight of Swords reversed, the Tower can indicate an injury to the ankle, knee, or foot, usually by tripping and/or falling. (The Hanged Man here can also mean traction: favoring an injured leg!) I always warn clients to take it easy when I see the chance of tripping and falling. And then they usually tell me they do walk too fast!

The Tower reversed can be a stroke, an embolism, inflammation, a rupture, or a sprain. Look at the Minor Arcana cards around it to figure out which part of the body might be affected and if a health issue is being indicated.

Death

When it comes to health, this card can mean a slowly developing problem. Reversed, it can mean something is not growing (anymore).

Hierophant

This card symbolizes traditional Western medicine. No faith healing here. Have the operation and be done with it! Take the prescription. Consult the guy who went to school for eight years.

The Hierophant reversed means nontraditional medicine: acupuncture, acupressure, herbology, iridology, reiki, and the like. If you see the Hierophant reversed and the Magician, this means the nontraditional method can be the way to go. But always encourage a client to go to a mainstream doctor, too.

A couple of years ago, one of my clients almost died of liver failure because he didn't want to have surgery and be on "those drugs" for the rest of his life. So he spent a year going to somebody who does Chinese medicine with herbs. And he nearly died. It was a miracle liver transplant (the Hierophant) that saved his life. (And I think the same thing happened to Steve Jobs, in reverse.)

The High Priestess

Since this card means the ideal to me, when I see it along with the Ace, King, or Queen of Swords, I think the client might be contemplating cosmetic surgery: the attempt to realize the physical ideal through surgery.

A lot of times I also get the message that this surgery is being considered by my female client so she can attract a man. I see the Queen of Cups reversed (no self-esteem or self-love) or the King of Cups reversed (the man who doesn't love). So I always point out that the surgery won't work to heal the psychological problems that make a woman think she needs to have an operation to be loved. Basically, breast augmentation and reduction, nose alteration, all the various lifts, liposuction...these are great *if* the people who have them just want to feel better when they look in the mirror. But that's it.

The Star

The Star reversed is depression. If the Devil is present, it is chronic depression, a serious thing, and it needs professional help.

Sometimes Temperance reversed appears with the Star reversed, and I think the client may be eating too much sugar (a depressant), drinking too much alcohol (a depressant), and/or taking antidepressant drugs—sometimes all at once.

I had a client once who decided she could eat as much candy as she wanted as long as she took her antidepressant. (What kind of doctor prescribes this?) So I looked for the tip-off cards: the Seven of Swords (guilt), no Kings in the spread (no men in her life), and the Three of Cups reversed (no friends or social life). The guilt told me she felt bad about all the sugar. I suggested she see a psychotherapist to deal with everything, most especially the absence of others and any kind of intimacy in her life.

The Moon

Upright or reversed, the Moon is the tarot equivalent of the womb, so its appearance can refer to conception. If this card appears along with the Sun (new life) and Temperance (healthy) and maybe the Ace of Pentacles reversed (planted seed), maybe conception is being predicted (and thus prevented, if that's what's desired).

The Moon next to the Five of Swords reversed, though, is abortion for me: anger/violence to the womb. When I see this, I always warn my clients about unwanted pregnancy, and I ask them to warn their sexually active friends.

If I see the Moon along with the Magician and maybe the Ace or King of Swords reversed, I tend to think it's a facilitated pregnancy (in vitro fertilization, for example). The Magician upright can also mean success.

The Moon along with the Devil can mean a serious problem in the reproductive system. With the Tower reversed (inflammation), it can be a fibroid. With Strength reversed, it can be an infection. And, of course, with the Magician upright, it's all curable.

The Moon with the Hierophant is a mental health professional.

The Moon with the Hermit is psychotherapy.

Judgment

Judgment reversed, in a health situation, can mean the client is not aware that something is wrong. If it's an illness, this can be dangerous. And if the Magician reversed appears as well, it can mean the client isn't aware that his or her doctor is not helping, or that he or she can't self-heal.

The Hanged Man

Upright, this card can indicate rest for the leg or foot.

The Hanged Man reversed can mean self-indulgence (not always a bad thing!).

Again, whether the implications are good or bad depends on the cards around it.

Now, please don't think that every time you see any of these cards it means sickness.

First you need to get a sense of the *totality* of somebody's life and where the details fit. You also have to have an inner impulse and aptitude to work in a therapeutic way. And you need a solid history of life experience.

But if you're dealing with a physical issue, you can't go wrong with what I'm telling you here.

CHAPTER 14

HEALTH AND THE MINOR ARCANA

In this chapter I explain how to use the Minor Arcana, either alone or in combination with the Major cards, to identify illness.

Many times, a Major Arcana card will appear along with a Minor Arcana card to indicate the presence of a health issue. In the last chapter I mentioned the Moon in conjunction with the Five of Swords reversed, for example, as indicating abortion for me. I also mentioned the Devil in conjunction with the Ten of Rods/Wands reversed as indicating a chronic fatigue condition.

Following is a list of the card combinations that have so far come to mean specific health issues to me. These definitions apply to health issues only. You too can use these successfully.

But as you work with people, *take note of the patterns that crop up for you.* With any luck at all, you'll start to notice that certain combinations always have the same accurate translation to a physical or psychological problem. So make a note of these, as they have now become part of your own tarot toolkit.

Cups

Four of Cups reversed: Succumbing to temptation (not able to resist that second slice of pie?).

Five of Cups: Spilled blood; blood pressure issue; circulatory problem; blood-related issue; cardiovascular system; cholesterol problem; anemia; bleeding.

Six of Cups: Family problem (genetic predisposition); congenital; hereditary.

Eight of Cups: Denial.

Knight of Cups reversed: Seductive issue involving food and/or drink or a person.

Pentacles

Ace of Pentacles: A single organ (like the liver, spleen, thyroid); a single birth; a pill, tablet, capsule.

Ace of Pentacles reversed: Conception; a growth; calcification; disc; cyst; sperm; egg; seed; pill, tablet, capsule; embolism; clot.

Two of Pentacles: Two organs (like the kidneys, breasts, lungs, eyes, ovaries); knees; twins.

Four of Pentacles: Dependency; crutch; clinging (to weight, for example).

Four of Pentacles reversed: No longer dependent; able to walk (literally or figuratively).

Seven of Pentacles: Dislocation; spinal disc problem; spine out of alignment.

Nine of Pentacles: It's possible the person can resolve the issue without professional help.

Knight of Pentacles reversed: Need help to work out the problem; see a professional; self-destructive tendency (maybe a noncompliant patient).

Rods/Wands

Ace of Rods/Wands: Penis; energy; vitality; protein; sperm count good.

Ace of Rods/Wands reversed: Low sperm motility; not able to impregnate; low sperm count; hair loss; protein deficiency; lack of energy.

Two of Rods/Wands reversed: Confusion; can't think clearly.

Five of Rods/Wands reversed: Problem solved; solving a problem.

Seven of Rods/Wands: Enough energy to fight with an advantage; having the advantage.

Seven of Rods/Wands reversed: Not enough energy to fight and have an advantage; no advantage.

Nine of Rods/Wands: Strength; strong immune system; good defenses.

Nine of Rods/Wands reversed: Not strong; giving up; compromised immune system; vulnerable to anything from colds to more serious problems; hair loss; protein deficiency.

Ten of Rods/Wands: Stamina; strength; longevity.

Ten of Rods/Wands reversed: Exhaustion; collapse; no energy; no strength; no stamina; hair loss; need protein; need iron; need nutritional supplements and a better diet; physical burnout.

Page of Rods/Wands reversed: Speech impediment; hearing impediment; throat problem.

Swords

Ace of Swords: Scalpel; hypodermic; syringe; surgery; injection; biopsy; invasive procedure; needles (as in acupuncture); probe.

Ace of Swords reversed: Same meanings as when the card is upright.

Three of Swords: Heart; cardiology; pain.

Three of Swords reversed: Heart; cardiology; pain.

Four of Swords: Recuperating; in the recovery room; getting strength back; in bed; laid up.

Four of Swords reversed: Recuperated; out of the recovery room; strong again; back to living.

Five of Swords: Relapse; remission not permanent; recidivism.

Five of Swords reversed: Pain; agony; knives; invasive metal equipment (but maybe in a negative sense, as this refers to "violence" to the body).

Seven of Swords: Guilt (can indicate a self-induced problem).

Seven of Swords reversed: Whatever is going on, the person has no guilt about it.

Eight of Swords reversed: Free (as from addiction).

Queen of Swords: Surgeon; physician; dentist.

Queen of Swords reversed: Surgeon; dentist; physician; but maybe an incompetent female doctor.

King of Swords: Surgeon; physician; dentist.

King of Swords reversed: Surgeon; dentist; physician; but maybe an incompetent male doctor.

The Cards in Combination

This book is mainly about using tarot cards the way we use words. I have talked about adding cards to a base card to form a complete thought or sentence. This means, of course, that there's usually no way to look at only one card and know everything.

The Devil

Devil and Temperance reversed: Alcoholism; hypoglycemia; diabetes; chronic stress.

Devil and Temperance reversed and Moon: Serious reproductive problem (with Magician reversed, may be incurable).

Devil and Temperance reversed and Two of Pentacles and Five of Swords: Asthma (and look for psychological markers).

Devil and Star reversed: Clinical depression (look for markers).

Devil and Hierophant: Treat with traditional medicine.

Devil and Hierophant reversed: Alternative measures and medicine, but should never be relied on if the situation is critical enough for the Devil to appear.

Devil and Justice reversed: Vertigo; illicit substance use; obesity; anorexia; bulimia.

Devil and Strength reversed: HIV; hugely serious infection.

Devil and Tower: Sudden serious attack.

Devil and Empress: A mother has a serious problem.

Devil and Emperor: A father has a serious problem.

Devil and Ace of Swords reversed: Surgery; biopsy.

Devil and Two of Pentacles: Breast cancer; lung cancer; serious kidney problem; chronic knee problem.

Devil and Two of Pentacles reversed: Alzheimer's disease; senility; chronic confusion.

Devil and Ace of Rods/Wands reversed: Chronic hair loss; alopecia; male sterility.

Devil and Tower and Two of Rods/Wands reversed: Stroke.

Devil and Nine of Rods/Wands reversed: Critically compromised immune system.

Devil and Ten of Rods/Wands reversed: Chronic fatigue; Guillain-Barre syndrome; dangerously exhausted.

Devil and Tower and Ten of Rods/Wands reversed: Collapse.

Devil and Page of Rods/Wands reversed: Chronic speech problem (e.g., stutter); laryngitis.

Devil and Six of Cups: Serious congenital issue; a family member has the issue.

Devil and King of Cups: Prostate problem.

Temperance

Temperance and Devil reversed: Healthy in a holistic sense.

Temperance and Lovers reversed: Need to adopt a healthier lifestyle (eating/drinking habits).

Temperance and Hanged Man and Strength: Health support groups; AA; NA; OA.

Temperance reversed and Lovers: Need to adopt a healthier lifestyle.

Temperance reversed and Moon: Hormonal problem; thyroid problem; menopause.

Temperance reversed and Devil and Ace of Swords reversed: Diabetes.

Temperance reversed and Justice: Illicit substance.

Temperance reversed and Five of Swords and Two of Pentacles: Emphysema (and also with the Devil).

Temperance and Seven of Swords: Illicit substance.

Temperance reversed and Knight of Swords reversed: Self-destructive habits.

Temperance and Four of Rods/Wands: Wellness center; gym; hospital; clinic; spa.

Temperance and Five of Rods/Wands: Gym; exercise; working out.

Temperance reversed and Lovers reversed and Devil and Two of Pentacles: Smoker; lung cancer.

Temperance and Three of Cups: Support group; workout partners; workout group.

Temperance reversed and Four of Cups: Trouble resisting too much food or drink; trouble resisting foods bad for you.

Temperance reversed and Two of Pentacles: Estrogen imbalance; reproductive hormone problem.

Strength

Strength and Devil: Person has what it takes to fight the serious problem.

Strength reversed and Devil: Serious/chronic infection; serious weakness; HIV.

Strength reversed and Devil and Moon: Serious/chronic bladder infection; chronic yeast infections.

Strength reversed and Temperance reversed: Sickness; no faith that the problem can be overcome (but with cancer and other such serious conditions, attitude is *crucial*).

Strength reversed and Devil and Two of Pentacles: Chronic bladder infection; chronic UTIs; ovarian cancer.

The Tower

Tower and Temperance reversed: Ulcer; stress reaction.

Tower and Knight of Swords reversed: Self-destructive aspect; tripping; falling; wrenching/spraining lower leg, ankle, foot.

Tower and Hanged Man and Knight of Swords reversed: Injury requiring traction or a cane or crutch; get off the foot; rest the leg.

Tower and Knight of Swords reversed and Four of Pentacles: Injury requires a wheelchair.

Tower and Devil and Two of Rods/Wands reversed: Stroke; cerebral aneurysm; brain event.

Tower and Devil and King or Queen of Rods/Wands reversed: Stroke.

Tower and Devil and Two of Pentacles: Pulmonary embolism.

Tower and Devil and Five of Cups: Sudden serious circulation-related problem.

Tower and Two of Pentacles: Mammogram; knee X-ray/MRI/CAT scan.

Tower and Temperance reversed: Arthritic flare-up.

Tower reversed and Ace of Swords reversed: Dental problem; drilling; root canal.

Tower and Nine of Swords and Five of Swords: Chronic headache; migraines.

Tower and High Priestess and Two of Pentacles: Laser surgery on the eyes.

Tower and High Priestess and Justice and Ace of Swords reversed: Liposuction.

Tower and Two of Rods/Wands reversed: Stroke.

Death

Death and Four of Swords reversed: Really slow recuperation.

The Star

Star reversed and Temperance reversed: Depression due to eating/drinking wrong (also with the Four of Cups); usually too much sugar in the diet.

Star reversed and Devil: Clinical depression requiring professional intervention; (may have nothing to do with diet).

Star reversed and Lovers and Four of Cups: Depression due to bad eating habits.

The Moon

Moon and Sun: Pregnancy.

Moon and World: Conception.

Moon and Hermit: Psychology; psychotherapy.

Moon and Devil: Serious female reproductive system problem.

Moon and Devil and Temperance reversed: Thyroid problem; liver problem (usually alcohol-related).

Moon and Temperance reversed: Menopause (also, with the Empress reversed).

Moon and Magician and Ace of Pentacles reversed: Medically facilitated pregnancy.

Moon and Ace of Pentacles reversed: Conception; seed planted.

Moon and Ace of Pentacles reversed and King or Queen of Swords: In vitro fertilization or a test-tube baby.

Moon and Devil and Two of Pentacles: Serious ovarian problem; serious breast problem.

Moon and Temperance and Ace of Swords reversed: Amniocentesis; breast biopsy; (also with the King or Queen of Swords reversed).

Moon and World reversed and Ace of Rods/Wands: No conception due to a sperm problem.

To Recap

When it comes to health and the Minor Arcana:

1. Keep an eye out for the following cards. The presence of one or more can point to a health issue.

   • If the Devil appears in the spread, alarm bells should go off, particularly if there's a health question involved.

- Temperance reversed means either too much of one thing and/or not enough of another.
- Remember, even too much of a good thing can be bad.
- The Star reversed is depression.
- The Moon is the female reproductive system.
- The Tower is sudden and usually appears with problems of sudden onset, like appendicitis and neurological events.
- The Lovers, upright or reversed, means that a lifestyle change is necessary, usually a switch to a better diet and exercise regimen.

2. The more medically applicable cards you see in a spread, the more likely there's a medical problem involved. Remember, it takes more than one card to paint a complete picture. How many tests does a doctor do to diagnose? More than one, for sure.

3. Start by learning the basic meanings of the cards, as I gave you in earlier chapters. Then, if you are meant to be a medical intuitive, you can progress to the information given in this chapter.

CHAPTER 15

The Mind–Body Connection

These days I doubt there's anybody who questions the fact that the body and mind are inextricably linked when it comes to health and health issues. In this chapter I talk about the principles behind this thinking. I also talk about the power of the mind to make or break us, how a reader can recognize mental health issues, and what a reader can do about them.

I mentioned earlier that diseases of the body can (and often do) show up with psychological symptoms.

Here's an example. There was a brilliant, visionary surgeon and teacher at Yale University named Dr. Bernie Siegel. He taught his cancer patients to pray and to visualize while also getting traditional medical treatment. His success rate with cancer was very good. (If you want to read something amazing, try his 1984 book *Love, Medicine & Miracles*. This is another work that'll stand the test of time.)

In this chapter I share with you what I've learned so far about the mind-body connection. I have read for many psychologists, psychotherapists, and psychiatrists over the years, and I'm told that I'm right on target in this aspect of my tarot practice.

And you can be too.

To me this connection is clearly evidenced when I consider the case of Lance Armstrong. I can only imagine what went through his mind when he was told he had cancer and only weeks to live.

Lance Armstrong is a long-distance cyclist. To me this requires grit, toughness of mind and body, and serious determination. This is a guy who'd have to be focused and physical, with serious stamina and endurance. I can just imagine him thinking at hearing the terrible news: *no way this is happening to me!* And really, there's no doubt in my mind that between his traditional cancer treatment and his attitude, this guy was able to erase cancer from his body.

Meanwhile, Western medicine has gotten so hung up on the tree that too many doctors ignore the roots! Until very recently, most doctors weren't even interested in what their patients were eating. (And, you know, we really *are* what we eat.)

Now, thank goodness, enlightenment is upon us. We're finally getting the message that our brains and our bodies are not on different planets. Many doctors are now telling us that attitude can make or break a recovery. That people who are depressed a lot are sick a lot. That people who don't care about eating right aren't the healthiest specimens on the block.

So this chapter is about what makes us tick. And about this I say that the only way to get over most serious psychological problems is to go to psychotherapy: to go to somebody trained to (1) ask the right questions and (2) not let you play games with yourself while avoiding the real (painful) issues.

What happens, for example, if a person suffering from alcoholism stops drinking but never tries to understand and heal the old pain he or she has been trying to anesthetize with shots and beers? Well, what happens is that this person never really *feels* anything. So, for example, somebody may stop using a substance but may never stop using people. I myself used to be that crutch in my personal life—a lot—until I went to therapy and learned *why* I was making that choice. And so I learned how not to be that used woman anymore.

𝒯𝒽𝑒 𝒥 𝒞𝒽𝒾𝓃𝑔 𝒮𝒶𝓎𝓈 𝒮𝑜𝓁𝓋𝑒 𝒶 𝒫𝓇𝑜𝒷𝓁𝑒𝓂 𝒶𝓉 𝓉𝒽𝑒 𝐵𝑒𝑔𝒾𝓃𝓃𝒾𝓃𝑔

Psychotherapy helps us get past the past so we can live the lives we dream of. If I'm seriously overweight, in this American culture that is based so much on looks, is the man of my dreams going to give me a second look? Maybe not.

Most guys aren't usually looking to see who's beautiful on the *inside*, at least not at first. I think guys are simply hard-wired to look first for the butterfly, not the caterpillar. And if I'm in great shape but spend eighteen hours a day working, seven days a week, when am I going to have time for the relationship I *say* I want? And if I spend most of my free time drinking or drunk, am I going to appeal to somebody who's healthy? No. No. And no.

So what I've observed in my practice as well as in life is that the men who actually want needy, desperate women are the men who don't know how to love and don't care to learn (and vice versa). They use, they discard, they move on. They're the guys (usually) who'll sleep with you and say whatever it takes to get laid, then you never hear from them again. And the women who actually want weak guys? They're the women who play mind and sex games to manipulate and control needy men. Both genders will take your hearts, both will take your trust, and many times both will take your money.

At one time or another, all of these types of people have found their way to my table.

So what a good reader needs to do when it comes to mental health issues is first to try and identify the problem, then *name the cause*, then suggest what can be done to fix things.

See, what I've discovered is that most of us know exactly what our problem is, and why it got started, and when. But most of us just don't have the courage right away to face the sad facts of our lives. So we go on, day after day, unhappy, not satisfied, allowing ourselves to be taken advantage of, settling about everything that really matters. Because of this, if we weren't angry already, we sure can become so.

This is amazing: I remember the exact moment I lit my first cigarette. I was angry at my mother. *This'll show her!* God knows how much damage I did to myself over too many years after that, smoking away like my life didn't depend on it.

Sometimes things can get so bad that I've seen people choose death over living any longer in a pain they can't name. So they get sick, finally, utterly unaware of it, *because they want to.* They just can't get away from hurting any other way. This is not just my opinion. I've seen it in cards and have read it in professional literature. Most times I see it when a woman is in a lifelong hell of a marriage. Finally, her spirit is broken and she "chooses" to get sick and die to get away from it all because she sees no other option.

This is how strong the mind is. And how *unconscious* some of our most important decisions can be. There are people out there who will disagree. There are professionals who will agree, at least in theory. All I can say is that this desire to get sick and die is not conscious, and I've seen it several times in readings.

Well, then, as a reader, if I can see this kind of despair coming, I can warn a client to find the courage to face his or her life, face the sadness and the pain, and be honest about who caused it. And because I can usually see what's coming down the road, I can then encourage my clients by telling them how things will be—if only they choose to find real help.

Who Wants a Reading?

Many times, the people who come to me are looking for some kind of magic. I'm sure they don't think of it that way, but—let's face it—if you're not willing to look really hard at what's wrong with your life, and if you prefer to trust a stranger with a bunch of picture cards to set you on the right path, then maybe you're just looking for magic. Shake the eight ball and all your problems are solved.

So what is one of the first things I try to do with clients when I see there is some emotional problem? I tell them *there is no magic.* I tell them that I'm not the answer to their problems. I tell them there is no answer outside of them. I tell them that the only way to arrive at last at any semblance of a peaceful, fulfilling life is to do the emotional housecleaning within that needs to be done.

See, this has happened more than once: somebody comes to me, and I see a lot of things, and I tell the client that he or she needs to *do* something to change these things. Well, if nothing is done and nothing gets changed, the next time that client comes to see me, the same cards will show up. When I discovered this, I learned so much. I learned that we just can't hide from ourselves, no matter how hard and how long we try.

You know, I read a *Dear Abby* column once in which a woman was upset. She wrote something like this: "All I want is to be married and have a family, and it seems that all I end up with is married men." Gee, I wonder how *that* happens. If this woman were at my table, I'd be showing her that she's *choosing* all those married guys, and I'd be telling her *why*, because I can see it, and I'd be suggesting counseling to get it all cleaned up.

It hurts not to be happy. It hurts worse to be in pain.

So my own reading style and content are designed to do two things: (1) inspire my clients to believe change is possible, and (2) guide them to a path toward that change and healing. What does this mean?

Well, for example, a person suffering from alcoholism needs both AA and psychotherapy to fully overcome the problem. The child of such a person needs both Al-Anon and psychotherapy. And so forth.

Addiction

That brings me, in turn, to a sad statistic: In thirty-five years, I've done maybe 25,000 readings for thousands of people, and I estimate that *at least a third* of these people are either addicted to something or come from families in which addiction runs strong. (I read the other day that 25 to 50 percent of Americans are *seriously* overweight. This issue is so pervasive that a former mayor of my city, New York, was trying to legislate good diets. We're a nation of crutch-seekers because we're a nation of people who are hurting.)

Some of my clients drink too much. Some eat too much. Some spend too much. Some gamble too much. Some are addicted to sex. Many are addicted to people who don't love them. And many times it's some combination of these. One of my clients once referred to a hateful lover as a "fix." Well, that's drug-use language, pure and simple. And I read recently about a woman who plays video poker in Atlantic City *eighteen hours a day* because, as she said of the machine, "It doesn't give me any problems." Well, this is anesthesia. Right?

Some of my clients work way too much. Working sixty hours or more a week is tough, but it does manage to distract us from that pain I'm talking about. The problem is it also *insulates us emotionally from those who are trying to love us.*

Another problem is that much addictive behavior goes unnoticed. A guy is praised for working eighty-hour weeks, but ask his wife and kids about the quality of their lives. Then there is the compulsive spender (and maybe hoarder). Big-time consumer and a credit card company's dream, right? Billions of dollars are spent on ad campaigns to get people to buy more. Casinos promise pie in the sky. Drug companies dispense millions of opioid doses without a second thought.

People who work with addicts tell me that addiction "masks the pain." But I say that, first, addiction anesthetizes the addict. If you can't feel, you can't be hurt. And whatever it takes to get to that place of non-feeling will win in the end.

Addiction and Tarot

I'm writing a lot here about this subject because I've noticed that addicts try to come for readings more often and more obsessively than other people. These are the clients who want me to make all their major decisions for them, the magical-thinking magic seekers. And I have to teach them that there's no way I will be their next fix.

See, your job as a reader is not to see the client every day or week or month and take the money and run. Your job is to help that client *not* to need to see you ever again. You don't want them to end up like my client who found a storefront fortuneteller instead of going for real help. She was nearly forever emotionally crippled by the experience.

So our job as readers is to see the problem and then identify the source in the past where it all started.

But there's a problem here: Psychotherapy isn't held in great regard by certain groups. Cops and politicians come to mind. God forbid somebody should admit to a "weakness." Also, people tend not to notice garden-variety emotional problems, like this one: "My mom didn't love me the way I needed when I was little, and now I 'never seem' to find love." Maybe someday there will be a *Lifetime* movie about this quiet little devastation everywhere around us. People unhappy everywhere. People hurting themselves in socially acceptable ways everywhere. No wonder there are so many therapists in the phone book.

Notlove (One Word)

There's been a lot of talk in the past maybe twenty years about "low self-esteem." Well, I can tell you exactly what this is.

It's the inability to love or be loved: it's the lack of *self*-love. If you didn't get what you needed emotionally as a little kid, from the person you looked to for it, there's no way you're going to be able to give it to yourself when you're thirty-three. It's that simple. *Esteem* is another word for "high regard." Nobody esteems things of no value. So if you don't have self-esteem, you don't feel you have any value. So this can't be about esteem anymore!

What it's about is not having been loved, because that is how we come to feel not valuable as people, and totally not lovable or worthy.

I saw a client once, a young woman whose father had sexually assaulted her when she was six. Well, this is what I saw in her cards: Not only did the man do this to her, *but she didn't feel as if she could tell her mother about it.*

And *that* is what damaged her totally. She hadn't been able to trust the only person she could have turned to. And I could see that mother in the reading. My client was right not to trust her.

When I told her all of this, she started to cry. What a relief to finally have it all out there in the open at last. The shame. The pain. The guilt. The beginnings of anger.

And this is why I say that a reader has to come from the heart, from a place of compassion and empathy. People come to us with issues far beyond our ability to fix them. But that doesn't mean we can't care, and it doesn't mean we still can't be of great service.

What I see as my biggest job is to inspire my clients to care about themselves.

Sometimes I fail.

And I can't tell you how many clients "can't remember" their childhoods. In fact, it's pretty much like arithmetic to me now. If you can't remember your childhood, it probably hurt too much to be there. It's that simple. But all that *un*remembered stuff is in there just the same, waiting to get out. One critical, tough backhand by life as an adult and we crumble.

A Little Story

Some years ago a woman named Caroline called me from Indiana. She'd been referred to me by another client.

It turns out that Caroline had been the victim of physical abuse all her life, from the time she was three years old. By the time she called me, she was at the end of her rope, miserable and *physically* ill.

But by the end of the first reading, an hour later, for the first time in her life Caroline finally understood her victimization. And she realized that she had the power to change things.

So she took herself to therapy, as we'd discussed.

For two years after that I'd hear from her now and then, progress reports. Then one amazing day came a note: Not only was she still in therapy, but now she was writing children's books—her life's dream. She was no longer physically ill. And, most important, she had persuaded her twenty-five-year-old daughter to go to therapy too. Caroline wrote that she'd told her daughter she'd been a bad mother to her. She said to her kid, "Now I'm working on loving my inner child. You go to therapy so you can too." It makes me cry to write this, it's so beautiful.

And *that* is what a competent, caring reader can do. If we're lucky.

The Law of Attraction

Readers who set out to be healers tend to attract people in trouble. So the only way you're going to be able to even start to recognize their problems is to know a little bit about how psychology works: Where pain comes from. What it means when somebody has a long list of bad relationships. What denial is. What repression is. Actually, it's all pretty simple once you get past the big words.

Over the years I've discovered that most of the psychological issues I see appear in the form of Minor Arcana cards. A pattern of bad relationships? The Five of Swords. Denial? The Eight of Cups. Repression? The Page of Rods/ Wands reversed. Frustration and/or anger? The Five of Swords reversed. The willingness to settle? The King and/or Queen of Cups reversed. Needing therapy? The Page of Cups reversed. Insecure? The Ten of Pentacles reversed. Codependent? The Knight of Pentacles reversed and/or the Four of Pentacles.

All of these can be psychological markers, the cards that can point you to what's really going on when your client either doesn't know or doesn't want to say. (And if my students and I are able to master this stuff with no background in psychology, most of you probably can too. I mean, it's just life, right?)

Now, many times a physical illness will show up in a reading alongside the psychological markers, which tells me that a holistic approach is needed. If you fix the physical symptom but not the underlying psychological cause, the problem will be back. I first noticed this connection a long time ago with fibromyalgia, and I've seen it many times since with multiple sclerosis and breast cancer.

This is fascinating: As I was revising this manuscript, for the *second* time I came across the *same* issue of Oprah Winfrey's *O Magazine*. The same issue: first in a doctor's office, then in the waiting room of my car mechanic, of all places. But you see, in this issue was an amazing story. A quite physically active woman had experienced a serious knee injury that had kept her basically unable to live her regular life for five years, I think it was. Finally, she couldn't stand it anymore. Nothing else had worked, so *she asked her knee* what *it* wanted. The answer that came to her was *run!*

The woman didn't hesitate. She went outside and figured, what the heck— and *she ran several miles.* From that moment on, it turns out, her knee was just fine.

I figure I'm supposed to tell you that story. I mean, who finds *O Magazine* in the waiting room of a car mechanic, never mind the very same issue months earlier in a doctor's waiting room? I confess, until then I'd not been familiar with this magazine. But I now think *O* might be a fantastic source of encouragement, inspiration, and practical how-to.

In the next chapter I share with you the cards and card combinations that can tell you who is hurting psychologically, from what, and why.

Finally, I've developed a broad definition of self-destructive behavior that's really simple: *If we're doing something, anything, that takes us in the opposite direction from where we say we want to go, we're being self-destructive.* This may seem an extreme attitude, but it's what I've learned from my clients over the years. As the saying goes, you can take this to the bank.

Think about it: The woman who wants a husband and family but only dates married men. The guy who desperately needs a job and manages to oversleep and miss a crucial interview. The person who leaves school *one credit short* of graduating.

Sure, something's wrong here. It all says: *This is how I can hurt myself. I choose it.*

Well, a good reader can be aware of this and see the clues everywhere in a reading when it comes to the self-destructive person—and can help accordingly.

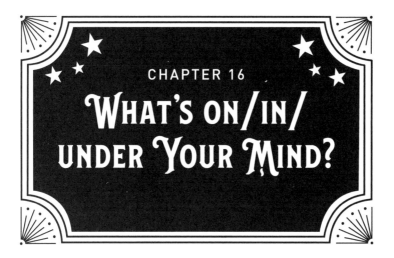

CHAPTER 16

What's on/in/ under Your Mind?

In this chapter I give you many of the card combinations I see in readings that tell me there may be a psychological problem at work.

Some of these combinations for identifying psychological disorders will look familiar. And that's because you did see them earlier—in the chapters on physical health and tarot.

So how can you tell the difference between one kind of problem and another? The biggest tip-off you'll ever get that you're looking at a psychological problem is that the Page of Cups reversed tends to appear. This means that the child who was not loved by the mother when little is still in there, inside your client, *still* trying to yell loud enough to be heard.

So "listen" for that Page.

Also, as a beginner, you may see the Hermit and the Moon, which are the combination for psychotherapy. With these, even though you're a beginner, you should get some idea that an emotional problem is present. Now, don't go hog-wild with this! I once discovered that for a while one of my students was telling everybody to go to therapy—whether they needed it or not! And while I suppose it's okay to err on the side of caution, what kind of help does a *well* person get from that? Not much. So wait until you really know what you're doing with tarot. When you're ready for this step, you won't have to think about it. A client will show up to teach you.

Also, you might take note of the body language of the cards. Is that Knight facing away from that Queen? Is that Queen turning her back on the King? It may or may not be relevant, but you should be aware that it could be. Try to learn to "get" the dynamic, the same way psychologists look at the body language in photographs to get an idea of the *true* relationships of the people pictured. Is one little boy standing apart from his family, for example?

Finally, lay the cards side by side for each of the following combinations and just look at them together, to "experience" the meanings.

Major Arcana Card Combinations

The Devil

Devil and Temperance reversed: Alcoholism/drug addiction/food addiction; health-threatening excesses; anorexia; bulimia.

Devil and Temperance reversed and Four of Cups: Dangerous overeating.

Devil and Temperance reversed and Justice reversed: Dangerous weight issue.

Devil and Six of Pentacles: Compulsive spending.

Devil and Seven of Swords and Six of Pentacles: Compulsive gambling.

Devil and King or Queen of Cups reversed: Addicted to people who can't or won't give emotionally.

Devil and Knight of Pentacles reversed: Codependency (almost always involves a partner with an active addiction).

Devil and Temperance reversed and Five or Ten of Rods/Wands: Workaholism.

Devil and Moon: Madness.

Temperance

Temperance: Mental, emotional, psychological, and spiritual health.

Temperance reversed: Excesses; stress; all-around poor health.

Temperance and Devil reversed: Healthy.

Temperance and Devil reversed and Hanged Man and Strength and Three of Cups: Addiction support group.

Temperance reversed and Seven of Swords: Guilt about excesses.

Strength

Strength: Putting up with an unhealthy situation; having faith in oneself.

Strength reversed: Despair; desperation; no faith; no faith in oneself.

Strength reversed and Temperance reversed: No self-control; out of control.

Strength reversed and Five of Swords reversed: Suicide (look for other cards to know if the act has been or will be completed); suicidal thoughts.

Strength reversed and Seven of Rods/Wands reversed: Chronic self-doubt.

Strength reversed and Seven of Rods/Wands reversed and Five of Swords: Compulsion.

The Star

Star: Hope; aspiration.

Star reversed: Depression.

Star reversed and Temperance reversed: Sugar-related depression (includes alcohol).

Star reversed and Seven of Swords: Depression and guilt.

The Moon

Moon: The subconscious; the unconscious; controlling mother; instincts.

Moon and Page of Cups reversed: (Controlling) mother doesn't love child.

Moon and Page of Rods/Wands reversed: (Controlling) mother doesn't listen to child.

Moon and Temperance reversed and Star reversed: Hormone-related depression.

Moon and Hermit: Psychotherapy; psychotherapist; psychology; psychiatry.

The Empress

Empress: Emotionally mature enough to be a wife and/or mother; the *idea* of being a wife and/or mother; the wife/mother archetype.

Empress reversed: Not a nurturing mother; immature mother; immature wife; not emotionally ready for marriage and/or motherhood.

Empress reversed and Page of Cups reversed: Child not emotionally nurtured by mother.

Empress reversed and Page of Rods/Wands reversed: Child not listened to by mother.

The Emperor

Emperor: Emotionally mature enough to be a husband and/or father; the *idea* of being a husband and/or father; the husband/father archetype.

Emperor reversed: Domineering; bully; immature father and/or husband; emotionally not ready for marriage and/or fatherhood.

Death

Death: Maturity; maturation; growth; outgrowing childhood conditioning.

The Hierophant

Hierophant: Tradition; traditional; first-generation; religious; by-the-book; orthodoxy (often reflects cultural influences on behavior and attitudes); mainstream.

Hierophant reversed: Cult; nontraditional; unorthodox; not mainstream.

The World

World: Closure; successful conclusion (note: divorce can be a successful conclusion to a terrible marriage).

World reversed: No closure; no successful conclusion.

The Fool

Fool: Not afraid to go in a new direction; not afraid of making a mistake; not afraid to fail; not afraid of the unknown.

Fool reversed: Afraid to fail; afraid of the unknown; afraid of being rash and making a mistake.

The Lovers

Lovers: Lifestyle change; change of habits; change of lifestyle and/or habits is needed (can apply to diet, alcohol intake, exercise regimen, work schedule, or geography of one's home); affecting leisure time and how it is spent.

Lovers reversed: Lifestyle change is needed; change of habits is needed.

The Chariot

Chariot: Having one's act together in general.

Chariot reversed: Not having one's act together in general.

Chariot reversed and Five of Swords reversed: Driving while angry (and dangerously).

The Tower

Tower: Trauma to the head.

Tower reversed: Conflict.

Tower reversed and Judgment reversed: Inner conflict of which one is unaware.

The Hanged Man

Hanged Man: Patient; sacrificing (can be too much = self-sacrificing).

Hanged Man and Strength: A religious faith in a higher power and/or faith in oneself.

Hanged Man reversed: Healthy self-interest; "When do I get what *I* want?"

Judgment

Judgment: Realizing (something).

Judgment reversed: Lack of awareness; not realizing something; needing to realize something (see other cards for what is in play here).

The High Priestess

High Priestess: The ideal; art; fine art; not settling.

High Priestess and Strength: Enough faith in oneself to hold out for the ideal (what one really wants).

High Priestess and Strength reversed: Not enough faith in oneself to hold out for the ideal.

High Priestess reversed: Settling; willing to settle (this never has a good outcome unless there is a *strategy* involved, a *reason* for settling).

High Priestess reversed and Ten of Rods/Wands: Settling now because there is a long-term plan in place.

The Magician

Magician: Having the power to change things; "I don't like what I see; I think I'll change it."

Magician reversed: No power to change things; manipulative; thinking one can "change" another person (this is *never* possible).

Usually, except when the Hermit and the Moon appear together, psychological and emotional problems show up in tarot as a combination of Major and Minor Arcana cards.

Minor Arcana Card Combinations

Cups

Ace of Cups: Having love to give.

Ace of Cups reversed: Having no love to give; emotionally empty.

Three of Cups: Having the support and nurturing of friends (usually women for women).

Three of Cups reversed: Needing the support and nurturing of friends (usually women).

Four of Cups reversed: Succumbing to temptation.

Four of Cups reversed and Seven of Swords: Guilt about succumbing to temptation.

Five of Cups: Regret; living in the past; not emotionally recovered from a loss.

Six of Cups: Supportive family in childhood; loving family in childhood.

Six of Cups reversed: The mother did not love the child in early life.

Seven of Cups: Dreams.

Seven of Cups reversed: Making one's dreams come true.

Eight of Cups: Denial; "I don't want to see it."

Page of Cups: Emotionally healthy child; healthy inner child; loved as a child; adult who has been through psychotherapy and healed.

Page of Cups reversed: Emotionally unhealthy child; unhealthy inner child; not loved as a child.

Page of Cups reversed and Five of Swords reversed: Abused child (usually the adult you're reading).

Page of Cups reversed and Five of Swords reversed and Justice reversed: Illegal abuse of child.

Page of Cups reversed and Devil and Knight of Cups reversed: Sexual abuse of child; molestation of child.

Page of Cups reversed and Devil and Knight of Cups reversed and Six/King/Queen of Cups reversed: Incest (other combinations may say this too).

Knight of Cups reversed: Seduction; a seducer.

Queen of Cups: Woman who loves herself; woman who won't settle; emotionally healthy woman; woman who knows she deserves to have what she wants/needs; woman who has been through psychotherapy.

Queen of Cups reversed: Woman who sells herself short; woman who doesn't love herself; woman who is not emotionally/psychologically healthy.

Queen of Cups reversed and King of Cups reversed: Woman who doesn't get loved by her partner, who cannot love.

Queen of Cups reversed and King of Pentacles: Woman who settles for a provider and the *illusion* of support.

Queen of Cups reversed and King of Pentacles reversed: Woman who settles for a man who will never be there for her.

King of Cups: Emotionally healthy man; man who can love.

King of Cups reversed: Man who cannot love; man who cannot feel; man who cannot give any partner what he or she needs emotionally.

Pentacles

Two of Pentacles: Coping; can handle things (not necessarily a good thing if the person is good at handling something that should be abandoned).

Two of Pentacles reversed: Can't cope; can't handle things (can be a good thing if the person can no longer deal with a bad thing).

Four of Pentacles: Dependency; crutch; crutch issue; fear of letting go.

Four of Pentacles reversed: Not dependent; letting go.

Five of Pentacles: Always feeling like an orphan; no emotional home; "Where do I belong?"

Five of Pentacles reversed: Finding where one belongs.

Seven of Pentacles: "What's the point?" "Why try?" "Why bother?" (a kind of giving up).

Nine of Pentacles: An independent person; alone but not lonely; complete without a partner; content to be alone until the *right* person comes along; content just to be alive. (This is my favorite card in the pack.)

Ten of Pentacles: Emotionally secure.

Ten of Pentacles reversed: Not emotionally secure.

Page of Pentacles and Five of Swords reversed and Eight of Swords: Learning disability (can also be with the Devil).

Knight of Pentacles: Self-sufficient; able to stand on one's own two feet emotionally; not dependent.

Knight of Pentacles reversed: Dependent; can't stand on one's own two feet emotionally; not self-sufficient.

Queen of Pentacles: Nurturing woman.

Queen of Pentacles reversed: A woman who is not nurturing.

King of Pentacles: A man willing to be relied on; a supportive man.

King of Pentacles reversed: A man not willing to be relied on; an unsupportive man; a man one cannot depend on.

Rods/Wands

Two of Rods/Wands reversed: Confused.

Four of Rods/Wands: Integration of the personality; all the psychological pieces in the right places.

Seven of Rods/Wands: Fighting for what one believes.

Seven of Rods/Wands reversed: Doubts; self-doubt.

Nine of Rods/Wands: Protecting and defending (see other cards to know what is at stake here).

Nine of Rods/Wands reversed: Throwing in the towel; giving up; giving up on oneself.

Ten of Rods/Wands reversed: Exhaustion; burnout.

Page of Rods/Wands reversed: Child not listened to; repression; child stops speaking.

Page of Rods/Wands reversed and Five of Swords reversed: Angry and repressed child; frustrated, with no outlet; repressed anger.

Page of Rods/Wands reversed and Devil: Autism.

Page of Rods/Wands reversed and Devil and Five of Swords: Stutter; language disability.

Knight of Rods/Wands reversed and Devil: Attention deficit disorder (can't focus).

Queen of Rods/Wands reversed: Not ready for marriage or motherhood; immature.

King of Rods/Wands reversed: Not ready for marriage or fatherhood; immature; unable/unwilling to commit.

Swords

Two of Swords: Unwilling to make a decision with emotional implications.

Two of Swords reversed: Making a decision with emotional implications.

Five of Swords: A pattern of failure; psychological pattern that is never good.

Five of Swords reversed: Anger; frustration; can mean a violent personality.

Five of Swords reversed and Three of Swords and Knight of Swords reversed and Page of Cups reversed: Post-traumatic stress disorder (in a child or an adult).

Six of Swords: Taking oneself away from pain or a bad situation.

Six of Swords reversed: Not taking oneself away from pain or a bad situation.

Seven of Swords: Feeling guilty; guilty.

Seven of Swords reversed: Not feeling guilty; not guilty.

Page of Swords reversed: One needs to make a decision; a decision needs to be made.

Knight of Swords reversed: Destructive; self-destructive; temper; violent.

Knight of Swords reversed and Seven of Swords and Justice: Illegal act of destruction.

Queen of Swords: Intellectual; not a hugging woman.

Queen of Swords reversed: Indecisive woman; cold mother; analytical mother; cruel mother; critical mother; unfeeling mother; angry mother; negative mother.

King of Swords reversed: Indecisive man; cruel man; hostile man; analytical man.

Interpreting the Card Combinations

Can you imagine the Page of Cups (a loving, sweet child) being born to the Queen of Swords reversed (a cold, critical woman)? Can you imagine how that child would *feel,* reaching out to be held and being told to get better grades instead? Can you imagine these two in a household with a King of Swords reversed (a cruel man) who drinks and rages (the Devil and the Five of Swords reversed)? Can you imagine the life of this poor little child? You don't have to know one thing about psychology to know that this child is being emotionally brutalized in that house (and maybe physically, too).

Now, as a reader, what you need to know is that the adult across the table from you could have been that little kid, and without therapy he or she will continue with self-abuse, taking over where his or her mother left off.

See, this person across from you is now all grown up and crying, not understanding how his or her life got to be such a mess. And you may be the very first person ever to offer real hope, solutions, a promise for the future.

This is what I do every day. This is what keeps me going sometimes. This is what you can do too. And this is why I work so hard to teach what I do, so others can be of true help too.

I can't tell you how many wounded children are walking around out there in adult bodies. (The teen suicide rate alone should make all of us stop and think. But we don't.)

Occasionally, though, it's the Queen of Swords reversed who's sitting across from me, the critical mother with a child not being loved. I see them both. I tell her that she's hurting her child. I risk the consequences to my career. (Kill the messenger?)

Finally, if you think you see a child being abused now somewhere in the life of your client, tell the client to get involved and call the police. No matter whose kid it is.

It is our adult responsibility to protect children.

The Client Who's in Therapy

When somebody comes to me and is already seeing a therapist, I recommend that the person discuss with the therapist what we speak about at my table. It's crucial to keep the therapist in the loop. Sometimes I see things and I know the client is deliberately hiding them from the therapist, so I tell the client to speak up. You can't get help if you don't talk about your problems. Again, there's no magic. Freud called it "talk therapy." So start talking!

The Worst Stuff

Now, when I think I see a psychiatric problem, I do the best I can. This stuff is reflective of chemical imbalances, brain issues. Psychiatric issues cannot be resolved through talk therapy alone. Many times they require medications. Sometimes it's clear to me that I'm reading someone with schizophrenia, for example, and that what I'm saying isn't totally computing. So in this case I tell the client to stay on his or her medications and I try to discourage the person from coming back to me. I don't want to take money from somebody I'm sure I can't help. It isn't right.

One More Thing about the Vulnerability of Kids

The twelve-year-old son of a friend called me one night some years ago. He wanted to talk with me about "spells and such, witchcraft." A half hour later, I was left feeling really uneasy.

It seems a lot of kids out there are being exposed to the occult in a very unhealthy way. It's in the schoolyard. It's on the internet. It's in movies.

But if it's dangerous for adults to be looking to curses and spells to solve their problems with other people, it's incredibly worse for young and unformed people to be doing it.

Magic! In the hands of competent adults, I have no problem here. I have friends who practice Wicca. They're mentally healthy and have a solid belief system.

But kids?

This conversation with my friend's son scared me. So I reported it all faithfully to my friend, so he could keep an eye on his son's mental health and social behavior. Parents need to be watchful, protective, and alert, today more than ever.

There are way too many *human* demons out there to worry about, never mind the vampire type, and a lot of them are lurking everywhere online.

The Reader's Mental Health

I once had a friend who was rector of a large Episcopalian parish in a major US city. He was telling me one day that every six months or so he had to go see his bishop to put somewhere all the pain his parishioners dumped on him. And so I asked him, "So you dump it all on the bishop? What does the bishop do?"

My friend said, "Every six months the bishop gets sick."

Nobody is immune to the physical and mental ramifications of dealing with hurting people every day. Doctors and trained healthcare professionals know they need to have a kind of invisible shield so all the sadness and pain doesn't get to them.

But I don't want a shield between my clients and me. They need my empathy and compassion in an active way. So the only thing I've found I can do as a reader is to take very good care of my physical self and to say a little prayer before I start working so I don't ever feel I'm (1) alone in this or (2) actually doing what I do without help from some source I cannot see or name.

You need to do the same.

And, by the way, if you're not functioning in a healthy way in your own life, you're probably not going to be able to function well in your work. I couldn't do half of what I do today if I hadn't gone to therapy myself long ago.

CHAPTER 17

ℛELATIONSHIPS AND ꞆAROT

Ɪn this chapter I give you many of the card combinations that tell me about love: the client's current status, problems with partners, joys and pain. And I'll say right off that some of you will notice other combinations as time goes on, as you work with the general public. Take note of these! Notice how often they show up *for you* to depict the same circumstances in various people's relationships.

All the notes you take will become part of your own tarot toolkit.

See, if we bring ourselves to readings—what we know, what we've learned, what we've experienced—then the cards we draw to address this stuff will reflect those things and inform us *in our own context* as a reader. This is what happened for me. It's what's happening for my students. So it can happen for you too.

Most relationship issues are going to show up for the reader in the form of the Minor Arcana cards. I suppose this is because the issues people face are mostly the day-to-day things.

The Major Arcana enter the relationship picture in the same way they enter other life issues. If you look at the basic and general meanings of all the Major cards, and you combine them with, say, the marriage card (the Ten of Cups), you can see pretty fast—without memorizing anything—just what is right or wrong with the marriage, proposed marriage, or relationship.

Love

So what *is* this thing called love, other than the subject matter of a million songs and poems and romance novels?

I've learned over the years from both my clients *and* tarot that our attitude toward *ourselves* is going to dictate to a huge degree how *other* people regard us and treat us:

If I respect myself, I will act accordingly and *command* the respect of all others who are *capable* of respecting somebody. I won't be drawing disrespectful people to me.

If I demean myself in my social behavior, I will attract people who demean me.

If I abuse myself, I will attract people who abuse me.

If I'm willing to settle, I'm going to choose accordingly, out of a *not*-conscious belief that I don't deserve more, can never have more, can never have what I dream of, can never have what I want most. And this is absolutely because I've been *taught* that I don't deserve *any* of what I want most.

I've had clients who described themselves to me as "stupid." Certainly they are not! But someone very important long ago *convinced* them that they are. (If we hear something enough times, it finally starts to be fact.) See, the somebodies who convinced them were seriously flawed people. They didn't love themselves, so how could they possibly love their offspring?

So if I feel I don't deserve to be loved, then I will attract people who won't love me. These people will usually say they do, but to far too many, love is just a word: a word that can be used to seduce; a word that can be used by somebody who wants what he or she wants, with zero true regard for me. Now, the client may not be conscious of this, but it never fails to show up in the cards. Lies, seduction, manipulation? Can't put anything over on a good reader. In this case, the word "love" becomes a weapon, and the shooters out there know exactly how to wield it and whom to aim it at.

Seeds

How do we form a self-image, a self-attitude? There are kids who cut themselves. There are kids who start drinking and smoking at ten years of age. There are kids who, as adults, consistently choose partners who won't give them what they need and want. These kids and these adults I see as being in crisis.

The cards confirm this.

So the million-dollar question becomes: *Why* do we harm ourselves in such dangerous and unhappy ways? *Why* do we feel we don't deserve what we really want in life? *Why* do so many of us settle: in relationships, in jobs, in life in general?

When the High Priestess falls reversed, I know this settling for less than the client wants is the case for that client. Likewise for the Queen of Cups reversed (the woman who sells herself short).

And so then I'm looking for the *why*. Why is this the case? The answer is always going to show up, and it's always going to be a card relating to the mother: the Moon, the Empress reversed, the Queen of Rods / Wands reversed, the Queen of Swords reversed. All of these represent various permutations of women who cannot nurture emotionally. *Cannot.*

Early on, I started trying to understand this. I mean, I knew I couldn't just go around accusing mothers of everything under the sun. After all, they were once just girls too, with their own wishes and dreams, right?

I eventually realized that somewhere along the line, too many of our mothers become thwarted: they choose partners who sabotage their dreams, they choose partners who diminish their sense of self-respect, they choose partners with addiction issues, and so forth.

What I've realized is that this kind of troubled mother was born to and raised by an equally troubled mother—and so on back across the generations. And I've learned that the *only* way to break this cycle is to go to psychotherapy and root out the anger, the shame, and the guilt we acquire very early in life. Without this, we'll simply continue to make bad choices. I smoked my first cigarette to get even with my mother. Really? So who ended up getting hurt?

When Are We Formed?

When it comes to our ability to truly feel and give love, I believe that ability is acquired (or not) before the age of five, or maybe even four. This ability or lack of ability to love comes right out of the early relationship with the mother. This, the cards have taught me. And I have absolutely no doubt at this point of the truth of it. Because when my readings are taken in this direction, they're accurate every single time.

One of the major problems here is a simple fact: we believe we're *supposed* to love and honor and respect and obey our mothers. *They* say so, religions say so, and even the courts seem to say so when they're hell-bent on returning children to mothers who haven't treated them well in the past. So mothers in most societies are put on a pedestal. They're goddesses, an archetype recognized all over the world. They're idealized as a species. In the cards, the Moon is the mother when it comes to the womb. But I've also learned that the Moon can signify the controlling, smothering mother when *other* cards fall to tell me the child inside my adult client is in crisis, that the child was never loved by the mother the way he or she *needed* to be. This child usually shows up as the Page of Cups reversed. The Page of Rods/Wands reversed shows up when the child never expressed his or her pain. I call this the repressed child.

My first experience with this was that young woman who came to me concerned that a relationship with a guy wasn't working out. Her cards showed two things: (a) she'd been sexually assaulted by her father when she was maybe six years old; *but* b) even *worse*, at that very young age she *already* knew she couldn't turn to her mother for help, for solace, for rescue. I could see it: A mother who didn't listen to her child (the Empress reversed) and a child who did not speak (the Page of Rods/Wands reversed). A mother codependent on her mate (the Knight of Pentacles reversed) and having no room in her heart to question anything he might do. A mother who no doubt identified with his success so she could basically justify her own existence, whose own dreams had been thwarted (the Queen of Cups reversed, the Seven of Cups, the Five of Swords). A woman with no real room in her heart for her child (the Page of Cups reversed).

And so I saw from this reading that in cases of father behavior that threatens or injures children, that behavior may be the smoking gun, but the *crime* is what the mothers *don't* do. (I have heard this a couple of times on the TV show *Law & Order,* and I'm grateful some of their writers are so astute.)

See, the kids know it. They know they can't turn to this person who is supposed to be there to love, nurture, and protect them. And so they learn, if they hear it, that the word "love" can be a lie when it comes from the mother.

Over the years I've been challenged on this point by a few clients, but they all had to eventually admit the truth. The second they were able to take their own mom down off that pedestal and think of her more like an equal than a perfect superior, they could see it. They could *feel* it. Many start to cry when they're with me. This is wonderful. They're finally making a true connection with their own little self.

John Bradshaw, the fabulous therapist I mentioned who's so great when it comes to treating addicts, has a method for enabling a person to get down to the source of his or her pain. I like it for everybody. The person he's working with pictures in his or her mind a moment in time when he or she was really little, and scared, and alone, and hurting. The person, as an adult now, walks into this scene, puts his or her arms around the little kid he or she was, and says something like, "I love you, I will be here for you, I will protect you. Nobody will ever do this to you again."

This moment can mark the resurrection of the child within and connecting that angry, injured little kid with the adult in whom he or she now lives. It can be the beginning of loving oneself. It's a powerful thing to do. It makes people cry, but not in a bad way.

How Does This All Happen, This Mother Thing?

I finally believe I understand what happens. Yes, it's a theory, but it feels exactly right. Before I'm born, I spend nine months inside a woman. It doesn't really matter how or why I got there. I'm there for nine months. During that very long time, I come to learn that this "container" of mine is protecting, nurturing, and holding me 24/7. In the womb, I have no name for this caring. It just is.

But then I'm born—and now that thing has a name. I am born with the *expectation* that this "love" will continue. But, see, it's physically impossible at the very least for *any* woman to meet that expectation of perfection. Nobody can live 24/7 for another person, right?

And once I got this, it made total sense what happens to us at the hands of most mothers, who, face it, are really just learning on the job. This may be true especially with the first child, but it holds for all the children. See, the learning curve isn't really about diapers and formulas. It's really about a mother learning how to *adapt her own life* to the needs of her child, not vice versa.

I've even had to lecture women at my table: "You have no right to ignore the emotional needs of your kid(s). Your *job* is to put them first." I mean, if we have a different man in our lives every five minutes, and we dote on these people to the exclusion of our children, it's just plain wrong. This is particularly so when one partner has an active addiction and the enabling partner is totally focused on the relationship. Everybody (the Devil in *both* cases) is putting the addiction first and everything and *everyone* else second. So if the "dry" spouse has to try very hard to be as attractive as the bottle, what emotional energy is left for anything or anybody else like the kids? Little to none is left, that's what. (Not to mention, nothing and nobody can ever be as attractive as an addiction.)

I need to say here that I'm not talking now about "low-life" scenarios. I'm talking about every single relationship on the planet in which there is alcoholism, excessive and unnecessary drug taking, compulsive gambling, workaholism, obesity, etc. If we're busy destroying ourselves on a daily basis, then we'll destroy our children before they've even had a chance to determine for themselves their self-worth, their value. And none of this has anything to do with intelligence, education, income, or social status.

The problem comes in when a kid—who is taught that Mommy is a goddess, right?—is rejected by the mommy. No love, no physical expression of gentle emotions comes from her. Only expectations and transaction ideas are conveyed, like "If you get an A, I will love you." Well, that's what the kid *hears*, even though those aren't the words. But it can never be so. That transaction is not about love, it's about demand. Maybe it's even about power. So the As come, but then even more As are expected. And so the kid who can get great grades starts to identify a successful transaction with love. (And God forbid the kid brings home a C.)

The fact is that love, the *true* emotion (even by the Christian definition), is *unconditional*. It is *not* a deal. There is no "if you do something, then I will do something else." Unconditional love (which, remember, we get in the womb) has no strings attached. (This might show up, for example, as the Ace of Cups next to the High Priestess: love and the ideal).

But, see, little kids are usually incredibly sensitive and perceptive, so they know pretty early on if they're not coming first with the mother. They become very aware that they don't get unconditional *anything* from their mom. (The degree of maternal failing, on a scale of one to ten, can be anything from simple emotional ignorance to outright physical and emotional abuse.) Many of these kids learn to entertain themselves. Many learn not to try to look to the mother for help and emotional support. All bury the anger they feel at being rejected but trapped in the home without a vent for that anger. Many start acting out, being disruptive. Many, mostly girls, start to cut themselves, to be able to control their own pain.

But all are in pain—a psychic pain, an emotional pain. And too many are made to feel guilt: "I let my mom down. Shame on me."

So I'm finally at the place in my life where I totally believe that our mothers need to *earn* our love. Great. But since most never got it themselves, how can *they* know what it is? They've married men who give them no more than their own mothers did. They suffer in silence, maybe for financial reasons. They stay, maybe because they're codependent. And they suffer.

Now comes the next problem for too many children. They think, "So how do I help Mommy feel better? What can I do to make her happy? *What am I doing wrong that she doesn't like me*, no matter what she says?" (This is especially true, I notice, of people with a Virgo sun sign or ascendant. They kind of have a mantra: "If I try really hard, my mommy will love me." And this ultimately gets translated in marriage and in the workplace to husband and boss. Nothing good can come of this.)

These little "helpful" children, of course, have no clue that the mothers may be suffering too. All are trying to operate in a context of limited information, along with that strong birth expectation that they'll be loved totally by the woman who held them within for nearly a year.

This is a recipe for disaster.

These women grow up feeling inadequate. Women whose mothers insulted them end up insulting themselves. Women grow up with this idea, "Well, if I wasn't good enough for my own *mother*, then what good am I?" This is not necessarily something we're aware of. But, like the operating system of a computer, it's in there *running our lives*. So then we're really about two or three years old, trying to function and succeed in an adult world. Is this scary or what? An angry little kid inside us is dictating all we do?

This can take many forms: "I don't care if my guy isn't nice to me; he's *my* guy." "I don't care about me. Why should I? So I'll just have another dozen doughnuts." "I don't care about my dreams, so I'll just stay in this job I hate until it's far too late to change." "I don't value myself or my money, so I'll just stuff it in pockets. (This is the theme of the second house of the astrological chart: how we value ourselves and our assets.)

The worst possible scenario in this area of life is the woman who doesn't value/love herself and sells herself short (the Queen of Cups reversed) next to the Emperor reversed (a domineering/bullying man in a marriage) and/or next to the King of Swords reversed (a nasty, critical, negative man). My heart goes out to this woman. And, look, if you also draw Justice (the law) and/or the Seven of Swords (dishonesty) and/or the Five of Swords reversed (anger), the nastiness in the home may be rising to the level of criminal assault.

But remember this: No matter what, the man is not the woman's worst problem. The woman's *willingness* to accept his neglect and/or his treatment is her problem. And as I said, this woman learned that from her own mother, one way or another. She learned that she doesn't matter in the grand scheme of things. I urge such a victim to go to therapy, *not* to talk about the man but to dig into the relationship with the mother when she was a little kid.

Many times for my clients, in fact, the Empress reversed, the Moon reversed, or the Queen of Rods/Wands reversed (all inadequate mothers) falls right next to the King of Cups reversed (the man who doesn't love). *It's the wife's mother and the man who are the matched set!* The client receives nothing she needs emotionally from either of them and never has. She doesn't know her two-year-old self sought this guy out to try and change him and prove that she's worth loving. (The Magician appearing, upright or reversed, tells me this was her secret agenda.) Without therapy, this woman will no doubt try her whole life to get men to "love" her, *and she will always choose the ones who (unconsciously) resemble her mother.* So she'll never, ever get what she needs.

Yes, I know the current mainstream thinking is that we "marry our fathers." Well, no, we don't. We men *and* women marry our mothers, at least the first time, and mostly this is not a good thing.

And one more thing needs to be said about relationships in which one person is not loved and/or is being emotionally and/or physically abused by the spouse or partner.

I tend to focus on the unloved woman issue because the vast majority of the thousands of clients I've seen over the years either *are* these women or are the children of these women.

But I've also had two instances in which the man was on the receiving end of neglect and abuse by the female spouse. And I've had more than a few instances in which the same emotional imbalance characterized a gay relationship.

So no matter the gender of the client, the reader needs to be alert to recognize the psychological markers (in tarot) that say: this is a very bad relationship. The reader needs to understand that *something inside the victim* has brought the person into the relationship and *kept* her or him there.

I am therefore alert to see the following cards:

- The Page of Cups reversed (the person not loved by the mother when little)
- The Knight of Pentacles reversed (the person does not believe she or he can survive without somebody there to lean on)
- The High Priestess (the person is all too willing to settle for less than she or he really wants and needs in a partner)
- The Knight of Swords (the self-destructive impulse that puts somebody in a bad relationship and leads to the choice to stay there)
- Strength reversed ("Why would anybody great even want me?")
- The Queen of Cups reversed (not self-loving)
- The King of Cups reversed (doesn't feel love)
- The Two of Cups reversed (no love in the relationship)
- The Devil (addiction potential in the unloving one)

Basically, just a couple of these cards show up and I know exactly what the whole relationship looks like. One person is hurting and needing, and the other could not care less.

In every single one of these cases, I urge the client to go to psychotherapy to understand her or his childhood relationship with the mother. Look, I know this isn't how we like to see moms in the US, but the result is that we're wrong too much of the time—and the victims are the kids.

I have to say this: On two occasions, the "bad" mother was actually my client, both women raising kids at the time of the readings. In both cases I had to tell the women they had "no right" to do to their kids what they were doing. And on a few occasions I've lectured men on how wrong it was what they were doing to their spouses (and, by extension, their kids).

The work we may be called on to do as psychics? It's fraught with peril, really. So we really need to know our stuff. Too many innocent and vulnerable people show up needing help. Most of the time they don't need psychic readings, they need psychotherapy. And first, the reader has to know how to recognize that.

But take heart!

If I could learn all this from the cards and from my clients, so can you.

Adoption

I've had a few clients over the years who were adopted children. And no matter how wonderful the adoptive mothers have been, the kids still suffer. They don't know why they were given up (thrown away?). They always have to wonder if they just weren't good enough or if they were a disappointment. Many of these kids grow up to feel abandoned, because, again, "Mommy is a goddess and she didn't want me." In my readings, this idea, the idea of being an orphan, shows up as the Five of Pentacles (searching out in the cold for "home").

In these cases, I look quickly to see if I can understand why the birth mother felt she had no choice but to give the kid up. This can always be found in the cards. And my clients tend to leave me with a sense of peace on the subject for the first time in their lives.

Maybe the mother was too young. Maybe she was alone and financially unable to raise a child. Maybe the mother thought somebody else could give her child a better life. Most of the birth mothers I see show up in the cards as continuing to think of the kids they had to give up long after the time they parted.

So if a client tells you (or you see) that he or she was adopted, just ask, "Have you always wondered why you were given up? Because we can look and try to see that." Most clients, if not all, will ask you to look.

What about Guys?

It's interesting. Maybe 90 percent of my clients have been female so far. Maybe 2 percent have been gay males. The rest have been guys of various sizes, shapes, colors, and careers.

And I've noticed along the way that most of these non-gay guys don't have this settling-for-whatever-they-can-get problem. At least not in relationships, anyway. I think maybe it's because women are raised to nurture (even those with careers) and men are raised to work. So the man has a very different attitude toward intimate relationships. Most aren't victims in the settling sense.

But very many of these guys from non-loving homes are the addicts among us. They feel like a failure, so they start to drink. They feel shame at letting their parents down, so they start to do drugs. They feel angry and want to "get over" on the world, so they start breaking the law any way they think they can get away with it.

Bottom line? I have come to believe that addicts are sociopaths. They cannot love, they do not feel emotion (although they may be able to successfully feign emotion), and they don't appreciate the pain they may be causing others. We all know at least one of these people. Many are married. And it's the wives and kids who end up suffering unless the individual goes to psychotherapy to understand and refeel the pain that started the addiction in the first place. (Therapy is needed because this stuff is always so buried/repressed that it needs to be dug out.) Without professional intervention, things do not change deep down for the addict.

I think this issue would be a great one to discuss with guys: "What is your attitude toward marriage? What is love?" Because I haven't had enough experience to know them and their deep issues the way I know about the women, who are willing to open up, admit they need help, and come looking for it. Guys won't even ask for directions, right? Yes, it's a joke, but there's such truth in this. They'd rather be lost!

Even now, in our "enlightened" society, many men are still being raised *not* to cry, *not* to show "weakness." But these men are people too, and they have tear ducts for a reason. Actually, I feel bad for guys in this sense. All this stuff to live up to? Impossible stuff? "You're the man of the house now," the mother says, and the kid is, like, seven years old. What a terrible, unreasonable burden.

This is interesting, though. I was able to observe a dynamic over time that was playing out in an office environment. A guy across the hall, young and earnest, worked directly for a man who was verbally abusive, mean, and negative all the time. The young guy was miserable. He was in effect the punching bag of this bad boss. But he stayed there a long time, taking it and trying to please.

So maybe men experience the settling thing in the career and work arenas and not so much in the intimate relationship arena.

Again, this is just a guess. I wish somebody out there would do a study: When, where, and why do men settle?

As for the gay guys who have come to me, many share the "female" attribute of settling, always trying really hard to prove their own worth to worthless partners. This, too, seems to be more in the workplace than at home, but gay men seem to be far more open emotionally.

Bottom line, in every relationship there's going to be a dominant person. I'm kind of resigned to that at this point. But selfishness (the King of Cups reversed), neglect, all kinds of abuse by another, self-abuse (the Knight of Swords reversed)…no way are any of these a sign of dominance. They are signs of victimization. And the partner willing to put up with it for too long is in need of psychotherapy.

The really interesting thing? If I see, for example, the Empress reversed or the Queen of Swords reversed (critical, cerebral mother, not emotional) and I see the Page of Cups *right-side up*, then I know my client is in therapy or has been. And it will be successful, because the Page position is upright.

Like I said, between my clients and tarot, I've learned so much about human nature and why we do what we do. For this reason, I ask my students to read a *Dear Abby*–type advice column every day and to watch *Dr. Phil* every chance they get—so they can get as much input as possible into what deeply troubles the people all around us.

Double-Edged Sword

And one final word about the Seven of Swords.

This card right-side up means deception, dishonesty, deceit, thievery. But it can *also* mean guilt. And once in a while it does. It will suddenly just *occur* to me. For example, if I see the Lovers and the Seven of Swords right-side up or reversed, I kind of intuit that the person has some lifestyle thing he or she feels guilty about and knows he or she needs to change. Most often this turns out to involve health issues, diets.

One more example: A woman who doesn't want to be married anymore (say, the Empress reversed) is secretly planning to leave the marriage (the Six of Swords). So she's maybe lying out of necessity and sneaking around. If the Seven of Swords shows up, it may just be *her own* guilty feeling at having to behave like that. As a new reader, you won't come across this (doubtful, anyway), but it's going to come in handy one day down the road when you're about to accuse somebody else of some nefarious thing and it's really the *client* who's feeling the guilt!

Love and the Major Arcana

When it comes to love and the Major Arcana:

- The High Priestess is the ideal and not settling. Reversed, it's settling.
- The Magician is the idea that a person can control or "change" another person. Not! And when it shows up reversed, this is the point.
- The Devil in "love" is a sick relationship (notlove). Reversed, it's healthy.
- Judgment is realizing something important. Reversed, it's not realizing something important.
- Death reversed is immaturity, usually referring to a partner.
- The World reversed means don't expect a successful conclusion or closure.
- Justice upright or reversed tells us a legal matter is entering the love picture.
- Strength reversed means not willing to tolerate something or somebody anymore.
- The Emperor and the Empress are people who are *emotionally mature* enough for marriage and parenthood. Reversed, they're not.
- The Tower reversed is some kind of conflict in the relationship.

Love and the Minor Arcana

Cups (the Love/Feelings Cards)

Ace of Cups reversed and Ten of Cups: No love in a marriage.

Ace of Cups and Ten of Cups reversed: One can love, but the marriage is dead.

Two of Cups and Ten of Cups: A loving marriage.

Two of Cups reversed: Two people not in love, no matter what they say.

Two of Cups reversed and Ten of Cups: The love has gone out of the marriage.

Three of Cups reversed and Ten of Cups upright or reversed: Usually means the wife needs the support of female friends.

Three of Rods/Wands reversed: A relationship has broken down.

Five of Cups: Somebody still regretting a past relationship is not ready for another relationship, especially marriage.

Seven of Cups and Ten of Cups: Dreaming of getting married.

Eight of Cups and Ten of Cups: In denial about the truth of a marriage.

Page of Cups reversed: These people will never choose well until they go to therapy and learn how they tick; otherwise, they will inevitably choose the wrong partners and *stay* with them.

Queen of Cups reversed: This woman will settle for men who are less than she really wants and needs (and so her relationships will never work the way she wants and needs them to).

King of Cups reversed: This man has no love to give, is unfeeling, can be emotionally selfish: not a good candidate for a long-term relationship of *any* kind.

King of Pentacles: When this card appears in a spread about a relationship, it probably means a woman is looking for security, a provider.

King of Pentacles reversed: This man has no interest in being anybody's provider; he won't be relied on in any big/important way.

Queen of Swords reversed: A critical, cold woman when in a relationship.

King of Swords reversed: A critical, cold man when in a relationship.

King of Swords reversed and Queen of Cups: An emotionally dangerous situation because the woman is sweet and the man is probably mean; usually, this Queen will fall upside down when the King of Swords is reversed (she's settling).

Knight of Pentacles reversed and Ten of Cups: In a marriage because one cannot stand on one's own two feet.

Nine of Pentacles reversed and Ten of Cups: Shared assets in a marriage.

Seven of Swords and Ten of Cups: Some kind of deception, dishonesty, and/or guilt in the marriage.

Five of Swords and Ten of Cups: A pattern of relationships that don't work.

Five of Swords reversed and Ten of Cups: Anger, frustration, and maybe violence in the marriage.

Nine of Rods/Wands reversed and Ten of Cups: Throwing in the towel on a marriage.

Four of Rods/Wands and Ten of Cups: A nice marital home environment.

Queen of Rods/Wands and Ten of Cups: This woman is willing to make a commitment.

King of Rods/Wands and Ten of Cups: This man is willing to make a commitment.

Queen of Rods/Wands reversed: This woman is unwilling to make a commitment.

King of Rods/Wands reversed: This man is unwilling to make a commitment. (Still, he may be married and infidelity might enter the picture.)

I need to point out here that it's impossible to itemize or name combinations for every single kind of emotional issue and relationship that can turn up at your door. But if you learn what's in this book, you can make a big dent in understanding most of what you will ever see. And you'll discover that so many of the things you used to think were unique are actually quite common! You just didn't realize it before.

CHAPTER 18
MONEY AND TAROT

In this chapter I talk about financial issues, assets, and tarot, including psychology and subconscious attitudes when it comes to money.

I'll say right now that most of the clients who come to me have money issues *as they relate to* relationships.

Maybe the husband (the Emperor reversed) will not let the wife have access to the family money. Maybe he's dictatorial about their assets and how they are spent. Maybe he's unreasonable and gets angry when the wife questions him (the King of Swords reversed, maybe with the Five of Swords reversed). Or maybe the woman in the relationship is a compulsive spender (the Six of Pentacles and the Devil) or a gambler (the Seven of Swords, the Six of Pentacles, the Devil). See, there's a *reason* why conflicts (the Tower reversed) over "money issues" are a major trigger of divorce. Again, how we each value ourselves and our assets can be in direct conflict in a relationship, and so the asset issue becomes a bone of contention. (The 1989 movie *The War of the Roses*, while hilarious, depicts an extreme version of what I'm talking about here.)

There is also the concept, usually maintained by the husband, that he's earning the money, so he decides how it gets spent. This attitude is usually derived from how he saw his father handle things. But if this guy marries a modern woman (a woman who wants a say in their financial life and who isn't dependent—the Knight of Pentacles reversed), look out.

In the case of divorce (Justice and the Ten of Cups, upright or reversed), alimony may be at issue. You will see that the King of Pentacles reversed has no interest in supporting the ex-wife and maybe the kids as well (Page(s) appear). We often see this guy with the Seven of Swords (deceit, thievery). Sure, he *should* give the woman money, but no way will he do this of his own accord.

One client a long time ago told me her husband was making a ton of money on Wall Street. They were getting divorced and about to go before a judge. The husband quit his job a week before the court date so he could stand up in court and say, "But your honor, I have no job, so how can I give her that?"

I kid you not. Such are the lengths some people will go to (men *and* women) to avoid a financial responsibility. It's outrageous and unethical and immoral (probably), but this stuff happens every day.

So when it comes to women and money, I always refer female clients to Suze Orman, whose work on the psychology of women and money is really useful. She warns, she teaches, she inspires. And, of course, men can benefit from her wisdom too.

Now, in the case of Pentacles in business, it may be that we're not getting what we should be for the work we're doing. In this case, you might see the Six of Pentacles (income) and the Seven of Swords (being shafted) and/or Justice reversed (not getting what one has earned).

Or maybe we get a raise? This may show up as the Six of Pentacles and the Six of Rods/Wands (victory).

Then there is the joint venture (the Nine of Pentacles reversed). The client draws the Ace of Pentacles (opportunity), the King of Pentacles reversed (not willing to be responsible), and the Eight of Pentacles reversed has fallen next to that King. Somebody is proposing a business partnership, but he's maybe not skilled enough to hold up his end, or your client won't be able to count on the person. If you also see the Seven of Swords (deception), it might be that the person making the proposal is an opportunist who needs money and isn't being honest about that little factoid. And even if the business is successful, the *other* partner (your client probably) will end up doing all the work.

So what looks like opportunity can really be an attempt at victimization.

In such a case, I urge my client to consult a good lawyer, just to be sure the proposal is on the up and up. And in writing. And signed. And I try to discourage clients from entering into business with *any* upside-down person. There will always be a very good reason the Kings and Queens fall reversed.

In all cases, though, where Pentacles enter into it, the relationships between money and other things may not be so clear-cut. The reader has to add cards until it's clear what the connections between things might be.

Moon and Six of Pentacles: Putting money in the bank or needing to.

Devil and Six of Pentacles: Compulsive spending.

Strength reversed and Six of Pentacles: Need to control spending.

High Priestess reversed and Six of Pentacles: Not an ideal income.

Ace of Pentacles and Eight of Pentacles: An opportunity for a challenging job.

Ace of Pentacles and Three of Pentacles: An opportunity for a high-level job.

Ace of Pentacles reversed: No opportunity.

Two of Pentacles and Six of Pentacles: Two sources of income; handling cash flow well.

Five of Pentacles and Six of Pentacles: Looking for a job to make money.

Five of Pentacles reversed: Not looking for a job.

Six of Pentacles: Healthy cash flow; money to spend.

Six of Pentacles reversed: Either no income or poor income.

Nine of Pentacles: Independence, entrepreneurship.

Nine of Pentacles reversed: A joint financial matter; shared asset (can be good or bad; the flavor of the situation is dependent on the cards that fall on and/or around it).

Ten of Pentacles: Security (emotional and/or financial).

Ten of Pentacles reversed: Insecurity (emotional and/or financial).

Page of Pentacles: Studying (for an adult, may be retraining, with a career goal in mind).

Ace of Rods/Wands and Five of Pentacles: Putting energy into a job search.

Ace of Rods/Wands and Six of Pentacles: Putting energy into earning money.

Nine of Rods/Wands in a Pentacle situation: Protecting what one has accomplished so far (for example, staying in a marriage because it would cost too much to leave, or staying in a job because otherwise savings would be eroded).

Five of Swords and Six of Pentacles: A pattern of failure in one's earning history.

Five of Swords and Eight of Pentacles reversed: A pattern of lousy jobs or of not working.

Seven of Swords and Six of Pentacles: Dishonesty around a financial matter.

Seven of Swords and Three or Eight of Pentacles: Can mean politics at the job.

Eight of Swords and Eight of Pentacles reversed: Trapped in a terrible job or a no-job scenario.

As I said, the above are some really commonplace scenarios when career and money issues enter the picture. But they're surely not the only ones.

So I urge the student to master the general meanings of all the cards and then see how they combine with other cards by practicing the adding cards exercises from chapter 7.

If you do this, you'll start to get a sense of how money and assets and work appear in readings.

Finally, many times clients have come to me about relationship issues when the clear indication in the cards is that they have serious *financial* issues. These tend to be single people not making enough or not working at all and not earning a dime. But instead of focusing on getting a job, they're putting all kinds of energy into relationship things. This is true mostly of young women. Often I see the King of Pentacles show up in this scenario, which tells me the client is thinking a partner will come along and assume the financial burden. Well, don't count on it.

Let me say right here that if a woman isn't in charge of her financial life, and if anything goes wrong in a relationship, she can lose everything. I have actually suggested to certain female clients with great jobs and bad marriages that they open a secret bank account in their name only.

We all need a financial cushion. And in this world today, even a little bit of one's own money can mean the difference between freedom and being trapped in totally painful jobs and/or relationships. So when I've seen bad/selfish men in the home and my client shows up as a self-sacrificing woman, I haven't hesitated to suggest this bit of deception: Just build a little nest egg. If things turn out great in the relationship after all, the woman can always put the money into the joint bank account. If the relationship disintegrates, she has something to leave with. At the very least, the woman leaves me understanding that she has power and can do *something*.

As for the case of leaving a job, I ask my clients to put money in the bank every chance they get while they're earning so if the job turns sour, they may have a shot at quitting without ending up homeless.

CHAPTER 19

LEARNING GAMES

I love this stuff. As I've tried to impress upon you, without a strong right-brain muscle, I believe we cannot be really psychic. But we can't do brain crunches and lifts, so what can we do? Here I share with you some things I've invented to exercise the right brain.

Okay, so now you have all the tools you need to do two kinds of readings: (1) the garden-variety fortunetelling kind having to do with love, money, and career; and (2) the targeting health issues kind. Using the seven-card spread and the card meanings I've given you, you can for sure do a credible job in category 1. And if you're meant to be in the healing group, you can start to learn to do a good job as well in category 2.

Again, many cards have more than one meaning. So how do you know which meaning is intended? Yes, you use the *write a tarot sentence* method, adding cards until things are clear and logical.

But, as I said earlier, you should *also* start working to develop the right hemisphere of your brain, so things will just "occur" to you after a while. You can actually get to a place where you're not even thinking, and words you had no idea you'd say are just spilling out of your mouth. After a while the instinct will be there, and you'll just say the right thing at the right time.

So here are some exercises to help you develop your right brain.

Absorb the Meanings of the Card Combinations

As you go through this book, each time I mention a combination of cards, lay those cards on the table and just look at them a moment, with the meanings in mind. You're teaching yourself by a kind of osmosis when you do this. Your *sub*conscious mind is picking up details and cues that may come in handy later. And you're seeing the images together, which is crucial to recognizing them together later. Meanwhile, the right hemisphere of your brain is kicking in.

Keep Your Head in the Clouds, Literally

Look at unstructured things and "see" other things there. See pictures, forms, faces, and the like in swirling marble, plywood, Formica countertops, etc. Basically, wherever there's chaos, look for things you recognize. It doesn't matter if they're real. What you're doing is forcing your brain to do something it was told a long time ago *not* to do: daydream, fantasize, imagine.

So just start seeing things in other things. Remember, when you were three this was easy! The idea is to get to the point where it's just as easy to do at thirty-three.

I've even been known to drag my students into my bathroom to take a look at the very clear faces that "happened" in the manufacturing process of the material around my sink, some kind of black stone with white swirls throughout.

But to get out of my john…I once had a discussion with a skeptic at a party about the validity of psychic work. The guy's point was that it's all bogus. So he says, "Fine, then, what do I do for a living?" I looked at the foam on the inside of his beer glass and "saw" a police officer and a desk. So I said, "You're a cop with a desk job." He nearly fell over. He *was* a cop with a desk job.

Then there are the images that can appear in cappuccino foam. And coffee grounds. And, yes, even tea leaves, and in the chocolate pudding swirls left on the bottom of the bowl.

Just start looking around, see what you can see, and find what isn't there. I promise that in many cases you'll be astonished.

See the Forest, Not the Trees

You're riding in a car, or on a train, or on a bus. You're waiting for the washing machine to stop. So take out your cards and sort of look at them, one at a time, but don't sit down and memorize them. Don't look carefully. Just let the images sink in below the level of consciousness. Look at the cards as if you're leafing through a magazine, looking at the pictures. This way, at some point in the future, if a detail is needed in a reading so you can be specific, the card with that detail will show up (trust me), because it was in your head all the time. Like somebody who's hypnotized, you'll be able to recall in the future what's sinking in now.

Imagine, for example, that one day the idea of Sweden may be important in a reading, and something in one of the cards will appear to tell you: *Sweden.* (Your subconscious mind already associates things with Sweden. It will be one of those things that will appear on the card to tell you.) It's not logical. But it doesn't have to be. It just has to work. And it does.

Work with Symbols

Ask for dreams before you go to sleep. Ask to understand them so you can get a handle on your own symbols. This way you can develop an ability to be conscious of the hidden things in yourself and you can learn how your own symbols work for you.

Look for Direct "Messages"

Notice shadow patterns on the sidewalk, the pattern of shells on a beach, the lines in your palm. You're looking for images you recognize: a star, a triangle, whatever. I once walked down an unfamiliar street asking if a certain relationship would last, and I soon came upon a red heart with a black slash painted through it on the sidewalk. Question answered. (Accurately, as it turned out.) Things like this are around us all the time. Start training yourself to notice.

Draw

Yes, draw. It doesn't matter if you suck at drawing. Make yourself do it anyway, five minutes a day. Result? Right brain activated and getting stronger.

Look into the Lives of Famous People

As I mentioned earlier, until you know what you're doing as a reader, you can attempt to look into anybody's life. Pick famous people whose stories you know or think you know.

Last week, one of my newer students decided to look at playwright Harold Pinter, and she was discouraged because what she was seeing didn't fit his life—*as she knew it.* Actually, what she was seeing made total sense for the life of a writer.

So I told her it doesn't matter about being accurate at the start. It only matters to start working with the cards. The more she works at it, the better and clearer her readings will be.

And this is crucial: Do not let your left brain (what you know) decide that you're wrong about what you see (right brain), as I did with the *I Ching* and Elizabeth Smart. Because maybe what you know is either not actually true or not the whole truth. You need to learn to trust yourself as a reader. And this comes only with experience and practice.

So be patient. And be in this for the long haul. It takes commitment to get good, as with most things.

Solve a Crime or Two

Another great tarot "game" is to use the cards to solve crimes. Who killed Kennedy? Where is Jimmy Hoffa? Who kidnapped the girl you just read about in the paper?

Ask your question and lay down the seven cards. The first and last cards will be crucial in the case of a crime, because they're the issue and the outcome. Do your best to understand what's going on, adding cards to each of the seven. (To start, I recommend "solving" a crime that has already been solved, so you can see how the process works for you.)

In your mind as you lay down cards is the question: *Who?*

If you can't see who did what, start a new spread. Lay down seven cards again and ask: *Why?* If you can nail the motive, you can usually nail the criminal. (Thank you, *Law & Order.*)

Here, the whole point is to see what cards appear for *you*, to be able to describe the facts you already know about the person you're investigating.

One word of warning here: Do *not* intrude in police investigations unless you're invited. You can't help, and you may even hurt the proceedings somehow. I recommend this exercise here only because it forces both hemispheres of your brain to work in tandem. Great detectives and physicians can do this. You can learn too, if you have the detecting/doctoring muscles.

Books and Movies

Try to read for characters in books or movies you know well. See what they look like to you when you use tarot. You may know, for example, that Raskolnikov was filled with guilt for his crime in *Crime and Punishment*. You may know that Chester Gillette was not filled with guilt for killing a pregnant Grace Brown long ago in *An American Tragedy* (based on a real-life crime). You know Harry Potter is a wizard. So check out characters using tarot. See what you can find. You're looking for the combinations that describe what you already know about a character and his or her actions.

And for you fiction writers out there, try using the cards to know what your own characters should or would do next. You might be surprised at where this takes you.

Basically, all these exercises, if done every day, will strengthen your right brain the way physical training strengthens muscle. If you're already an artist, your intuitive sense is probably already developed to a degree. But if you're not, you have some catching up to do.

So just relax and, basically, let yourself be a kid again.

Or maybe even for the first time?

CHAPTER 20
Homework (Ugh!)

Somewhere along the line as a tarot teacher, I came up with the idea of asking my students to translate English language words and phrases into tarot cards. I discovered that this is a really effective way of getting students to master the card meanings and engage both hemispheres of the brain at the same time.

It goes like this: I give you some words, maybe a sentence, and you tell me the words *using tarot cards to express them*.

For example, if I say "house," you give me the Four of Rods/Wands.

If I say "making money at a masterful job," you give me the Six of Pentacles and the Three of Pentacles.

You can use as many cards as you need to get the exact message across.

I should point out here that there may be more than one correct set of cards to express any given idea. Remember, we all bring *ourselves* to this process. The only rule here is that somebody else needs to get the original words when they see the cards you choose.

So here is some homework to get you started: phrases, clauses, and sentences to challenge you. Once you've mastered all of these to your own satisfaction, try sentences at random: from the newspaper, TV, books. It doesn't really matter what words are involved. It only matters that you are doing the exercise and working the left *and* the right brain at the same time. (My answers are at the end of this chapter.)

1. Overcoming an addiction.
2. Accepting an offer of a low-skilled job with no growth.
3. Angry man.
4. On public assistance (or social security or unemployment).
5. News is coming from a friend.

6. Getting together with friends from work.
7. Mother ignoring her child.
8. Man not ready for commitment to marriage.
9. Man not ready for responsibilities of marriage.
10. Criminal lawyer.

11. Dreaming of being a priest.
12. Time to look for a new job.
13. Looking for the right job.
14. She says, "What's the point of trying to make my marriage work?"
15. Working two jobs, one of which is a civil service job.

16. Flying to another country.
17. Computer crashes.
18. Gifted in an artistic way.
19. The psychic predicts a happy marriage.
20. Father won't pay for kids' schooling.

21. Investing in education.
22. Mother is an alcoholic.
23. Architect of houses.
24. Attempted murder.
25. Dreaming of being an entrepreneur.

26. Dreams while one is sleeping.

27. Feeling guilty about a joint financial matter.

28. She won't repay the money she borrows.

29. The ideal male love.

30. A sister or brother at a distance.

31. A sister is coming from another country.

32. Three sisters.

33. He says, "I want to be a doctor."

34. Medical school.

35. Fundraising for a charitable organization.

36. Adopting a foreign child.

37. Burnout at work.

38. Deciding to learn to drive.

39. She says, "I'm going on a diet."

40. An idea for a novel leads to taking a writing class.

41. Working on a relationship.

42. The marriage is over and a divorce is going to happen.

43. Alimony and / or child support.

44. The man has a congenital heart condition.

45. Looking for a house to buy.

46. She sings for a living.

47. She works freelance.

48. Making money from two sources.

49. Getting out of a bad situation into a worse one.

50. Deciding to leave home and go to college.

51. The therapist is happily married.

52. The girl isn't ready to be a mother and terminates the pregnancy.

53. Buying a computer or TV.

54. Justice denied.

55. The court will rule in your favor.

56. The ex-husband hides assets from his ex-wife.

57. Breaking an addiction with the help of a support group.

58. Road rage.

59. Falling and twisting an ankle.

60. Surgery for spine out of alignment.

61. Family member gets fired.

62. She is emotionally insecure and needy.

63. Not earning enough to stand on one's own two feet.

64. Wanting to run away from home but afraid to cross the street.

65. "I quit!" There's too much politics in this office.

66. The man says, "I don't love you anymore."

67. The man doesn't know how to love.

68. The child grew up in an emotional battlefield.

69. Focus on making a career change by going to school.

70. Need to focus on making money.

71. Police officer.

72. "My marriage is unhappy and I don't want to admit it."

73. The man is having knee surgery.

74. Laser surgery on eyes.

75. Injecting heroin or cocaine.

76. Time to make a brand-new start.

77. The dog is sick.

78. Healthy and happy.

79. Needing to eat better and work out.

80. A seductive situation will have a bad outcome.

81. She is so unhappy.

82. Controlling mother and controlling husband.

83. "I love to shock people!"

84. Having faith in God but not in organized religion.

85. The entrepreneur is a chef.

86. The woman comes from a country at war.

87. The air-sign man (Gemini, Libra, Aquarius) is confused.

88. It is a victory to leave a relationship where there is no love.

89. Throwing in the towel.

90. The woman sells herself short/by settling/for a bad marriage/to a man who doesn't love her/because she needs someone to take care of her/because she can't stand on her own two feet/because her mother didn't care about her when she was little.

(I gave you this one so you can see how a big idea is broken down into its parts.)

91. Conflict at a good job.

92. No longer in love with someone for whom you were settling in the first place.

93. She says, "I can stand on my own two feet and I dream of being a mother."

94. The ideal government.

95. The domineering father does not listen to his kid's dreams.

96. Throwing in the towel on being friends with a dishonest lifelong friend.

97. Not afraid of making a completely new start and going after a huge dream.

98. Being tempted to settle.

99. Taking oneself away from a disruptive work situation.

100. Not able to handle a bad marriage.

101. Demanding more than one has been getting at a learning-curve job because one deserves it.

102. The earth-sign woman (Taurus, Virgo, Capricorn) drives while angry and risks an accident.

103. "Eventually I will find a job that pays well."

104. Out of the blue, a marriage proposal.

105. Resolution of the problem is imminent.

106. Aspiring to be president of the United States.

107. Feeling guilty about one's weight.

108. The student is frustrated.

109. Television is tedious.

110. Someone contemplates a long-distance trip to another country.

You may have noticed something. If you do this right, you don't need to worry about words like *but*, *and*, or *because*, because, as you read earlier, what you've "written" with the cards, what you say out loud, will make no sense with the wrong connective.

I know how challenging this exercise is. I also know how valuable it is. My students all really enjoy it (especially the type-A ones!). I hope you will too.

Answers

1. Devil reversed and Strength. Devil reversed and Temperance.

2. Four of Cups reversed, Eight of Pentacles reversed, and Ace of Rods/ Wands reversed.

3. Any King and Five of Swords reversed.

4. Six of Pentacles and Hierophant

5. Eight of Rods/Wands and Three of Cups. Page of Rods/Wands and Three of Cups.

6. Three of Cups and Three of Pentacles. Three of Cups and Eight of Pentacles.

7. Empress reversed and Page of Rods/Wands reversed. Queen of Rods/ Wands reversed and Page of Rods/Wands reversed.

8. King of Rods/Wands reversed.

9. King of Pentacles reversed.

10. King of Swords and Justice (and Hierophant if the lawyer is a district attorney).

11. Seven of Cups and Hanged Man and Strength and Hierophant.

12. Wheel of Fortune and Five of Pentacles.

13. Five of Pentacles and Queen of Pentacles.

14. Any Queen and Seven of Pentacles and Ten of Cups reversed.

15. Two of Pentacles and Hierophant.

16. Eight of Rods/Wands and Hierophant.

17. Tower and Moon and Ten of Rods/Wands reversed.

18. Magician and High Priestess.

19. Moon and High Priestess and Ten of Cups.

20. King of Pentacles reversed and Page of Pentacles.

21. Six of Pentacles and Page of Pentacles.

22. Empress reversed and Devil and Temperance reversed. Queen of Rods/ Wands reversed and Devil and Temperance reversed.

23. Magician and Four of Rods/Wands.

24. Five of Swords reversed and Justice and Knight of Swords reversed. Five of Swords reversed and Justice reversed and Knight of Swords reversed.

25. Seven of Cups and Nine of Pentacles.

26. Moon.

27. Seven of Swords and Nine of Pentacles reversed.

28. Any Queen and Seven of Swords and Nine of Pentacles reversed.

29. King of Cups and High Priestess.

30. Queen or King of Rods/Wands and Three of Rods/Wands. Six of Cups and Three of Rods/Wands.

31. Any Queen and Eight of Rods/Wands and Hierophant.

32. Six of Cups and Three of Cups.

33. Page of Rods/Wands and Seven of Cups and Magician and Temperance.

34. Page of Pentacles and Magician and Temperance.

35. Six of Pentacles and Temperance.

36. Hierophant and Justice and Page of Cups.

37. Ten of Rods/Wands reversed and Three (or Eight) of Pentacles.

38. Ace (or Page) of Swords and Chariot and Page of Pentacles.

39. Any Queen and Lovers and Justice and Temperance (or Strength).

40. Ace of Rods/Wands and Page of Rods/Wands and Page of Pentacles.

41. Eight of Pentacles and Three of Rods/Wands.

42. Ten of Cups reversed and Justice.

43. Ten of Cups reversed and Justice and Six of Pentacles.

44. Any King and Three of Swords and Six of Cups.

45. Five of Pentacles and Six of Pentacles.

46. Any Queen and Page of Rods/Wands and Six of Pentacles.

47. Any Queen and Hierophant reversed and Six of Pentacles.

48. Two of Pentacles.

49. Six of Swords and Three of Swords.

50. Lovers and Four of Rods/Wands reversed and Page of Pentacles.

51. Moon and Hermit and Ten of Cups.

52. Queen of Rods/Wands reversed and Moon and Five of Swords reversed. Empress reversed and Moon and Five of Swords reversed.

53. Six of Pentacles and Tower and Moon.

54. Justice reversed.

55. Hierophant and Justice.

56. King of Pentacles reversed and Queen of Cups reversed and Ten of Cups reversed and Justice and Seven of Swords.

57. Devil reversed and Temperance and Three of Cups.

58. Chariot reversed and Five of Swords reversed.

59. Knight of Swords reversed and Tower reversed.

60. Ace of Swords (or King/Queen of Swords) and Seven of Pentacles.

61. Six of Cups and Tower.

62. Queen of Cups reversed and Ten of Pentacles reversed.

63. Six of Pentacles reversed and Knight of Pentacles reversed.

64. Seven of Cups and Lovers and Fool reversed.

65. Tower and Seven of Swords and Eight (or Three) of Pentacles.

66. Any King and Page of Rods/Wands and Two of Cups reversed.

67. King of Cups reversed.

68. Page of Cups reversed and Six of Cups reversed and Five of Swords reversed.

69. Knight of Rods/Wands and Eight of Pentacles and Page of Pentacles.

70. Knight of Rods/Wands and Six of Pentacles.

71. Any King/Queen and Hierophant and Seven of Swords. Any King/Queen and Justice and Seven of Swords.

72. Ten of Cups reversed and Eight of Cups. Ten of Cups reversed and Eight of Cups and Three of Swords.

73. Any King and Ace of Swords and Two of Pentacles and Devil.

74. Tower and High Priestess and Magician and Two of Pentacles.

75. Ace of Swords reversed and Temperance reversed (and maybe Justice reversed). Knight of Swords reversed and Temperance reversed (and maybe Justice reversed).

76. Fool. Fool and Wheel of Fortune.

77. Moon and Devil. Moon and Temperance reversed.

78. Temperance and Nine of Cups.

79. Lovers and Temperance reversed and Five of Rods/Wands. Lovers reversed and Temperance reversed and Five of Rods/Wands.

80. Knight of Cups reversed and Three of Swords. Knight of Cups reversed and Nine of Swords.

81. Any Queen and Nine of Swords.

82. Moon and Emperor reversed.

83. Hierophant reversed and Tower.

84. Strength and Hanged Man and Hierophant reversed.

85. Nine of Pentacles and Temperance.

86. Any Queen and Eight of Rods/Wands and Hierophant and Five of Swords reversed.

87. King of Swords and Two of Rods/Wands reversed.

88. Six of Rods/Wands and Six of Swords and Two of Cups reversed.

89. Nine of Rods/Wands reversed.

90. Queen of Cups reversed/High Priestess reversed/Ten of Cups reversed/King of Cups reversed/King of Pentacles/Knight of Pentacles reversed/Page of Cups reversed.

91. Tower reversed and Eight of Pentacles. Tower reversed and Three of Pentacles.

92. Two of Cups reversed and High Priestess reversed and Three of Rods/Wands reversed.

93. Any Queen and Page of Rods/Wands and Knight of Pentacles and Seven of Cups and Empress.

94. High Priestess and Hierophant.

95. Emperor reversed and Page of Rods/Wands reversed and Seven of Cups.

96. Nine of Rods/Wands reversed and Seven of Swords and Six of Cups.

97. Fool and Star.

98. Four of Cups and High Priestess reversed.

99. Six of Swords and Four of Rods/Wands reversed.

100. Two of Pentacles reversed and Ten of Cups reversed.

101. Hanged Man reversed and Eight of Pentacles.

102. Queen of Pentacles and Chariot reversed and Five of Swords reversed.

103. Ten of Rods/Wands and Five of Pentacles reversed and Six of Pentacles.

104. Knight of Swords and Four of Cups and Ten of Cups.

105. Five of Rods/Wands reversed and Eight of Rods/Wands.

106. Star and Emperor and Hierophant and Moon. (The Moon "rules" the sign of Cancer, which is July 4, which is the birth date of the US.)

107. Seven of Swords and Temperance reversed.

108. Page of Pentacles and Five of Swords reversed.

109. Moon and Tower and Seven of Pentacles reversed.

110. Knight of Cups and Eight of Rods/Wands and Hierophant.

Okay, good for you, no matter how you did!

Now, every couple of months, try these all again. If you think you didn't do so well the first time through, you'll find that you can do better as time goes on.

CHAPTER 21

Ethics 101 for the
Professional Reader

In this chapter I offer the "rules" and guidelines by which I operate and maintain a sense of professionalism as a professional psychic. Here, too, are issues too delicate to be ignored in this book but maybe also too delicate to be dealt with in a professional setting. As with all ethical matters, in the end, whether you pay attention here is totally up to you, though I sure hope you will.

On Death and Dying

I'm including this coverage here because too many people have asked me over the years not about their own deaths but about the life spans of people they love and people they totally don't love. This means that if you learn to do what I do, you may be confronted by the same thing.

You know, every once in a while during a reading I see somebody in the cards who's in the afterlife. And I usually feel that this person's mission *after* death is to watch over a loved one still here on Earth until that loved one's life is healed or at least under control. Usually these are mothers who weren't so great to their kids when they were alive and who seem to be sticking around now, after death, to do what they didn't do before: love and protect their kids (my clients).

And in readings, on rare occasions the dead show up (actually, ten times in 25,000 readings) because they have a message for the client. One time it was a father telling his daughter, "You can do it!" Of course, this may be my fantasy, but when I've had these experiences in readings, the clients have confirmed my sense of things. All of them have felt the presence of the particular person who I think has come to say hello and encourage them somehow.

So over time I've learned that this little pack of seventy-eight tarot cards can also tell the story of the universe, one person at a time. It can represent the life of a soul, tell the story of a soul. This is also why, maybe once in a thousand readings, I think I'm glimpsing a past life. At such times I literally caution my client to take what I'm saying with a grain of salt. For sure, none of it can be proved. Still, in several cases, the *few* times this has happened in my career, the client had *already* sensed a life in the place and time I was describing.

But what is the absolute most important thing I can say about past lives, while I'm on the subject?

If your client claims that life sucks, if the client is always unhappy, if the client is depressed, if the client always seems to be victimized…Whatever the negative situation is, the client needs to know it has *not* been caused by something in a past life. No! The fact is the problem has been caused by somebody or something *in this life*.

I've had a lot of clients over the years desperately trying to blame previous existences for the pain done to them in this one, especially by denying the reality of their childhood in this life. This is just dangerous, because it means that we're not looking at our own lives and our own betrayals and our own painful experiences in order to fix them.

Yes, I do believe that we can access information about past lives through hypnotic regression, but I also believe that whatever we find there *we will find here too*. As others do, I believe we come into this life with unresolved issues from the past. These are then *duplicated* somehow in this life.

So, look, it's the stuff of *this* life that's the cause of our pain in this life. And this is what needs fixing. You won't get better in 2020 by "remembering" what may or may not have happened in 1500.

Finally, I didn't "see" my first spirit in the cards until I'd been reading professionally for maybe fifteen years. And there's nothing I can do now to make this happen. People "come" or they don't. And it's also entirely possible that I've missed many along the way besides the ten or so I can be sure of. So if you try to use tarot to contact the dead, it may work because you have a particular gift. But, more likely, it won't work at all. Everything takes time, and what is ours comes to us. So just work hard and wait to see what comes to you.

Misusing Tarot

Now I need to say something about the criminal aspect, the immoral aspect, the unethical aspect of tarot, or any oracle for that matter, in the wrong hands.

I once overheard a "reader" tell a man, "No, you don't need to see a doctor; it's just a little lump."

Oh my god.

And this is the same "reader" who, it seems, had done some stock market "advising" before that for a different client, who'd ended up losing his shirt following her "psychic" instructions.

Somebody please steal her cards.

My Model

I long ago modeled my practice on that of the psychotherapist when it comes to confidentiality. I tell nobody for any reason who has consulted me. My clients can shout it to the rooftops. But I believe it is my responsibility to keep my mouth shut, and so I do.

On the other hand, I do my own thing when it comes to using my own life as parable. While most psychotherapists are trained to listen and not share, I don't have to operate under such constraints. In fact, I've discovered that being able to explain to a client that I have been a total screw-up in life at times enables me to make a simply human connection. The client doesn't feel lectured. All good.

Don't Pretend to Know What You Don't Know

There are so many people out there billing themselves as "psychics," it's kind of scary. As a matter of fact, it took me many years to even admit that maybe I had some kind of gift.

So be humble. Be discreet. Don't lie to your clients. Don't pretend you know what you don't.

If you're honest and direct and compassionate, you'll be the kind of reader they'll want to recommend.

CONCLUSION

So there you go. You don't know as much as I do (not yet anyway), but I've tried hard here to give you a really good start to truly understanding and speaking the language of tarot. Now you can begin reading tarot cards in the same way you read newspapers and books. No more guesswork! Or almost none, anyway. The fact is that you'll be able to trust what you see and say, and as time goes on and you progress, what you see will become deeper and more detailed.

If you use this book the way it's intended—if you work hard to learn the meanings of the cards right-side up and reversed; if you practice setting free and developing your right brain (with the creative exercises); if you approach each person you read as someone in need of help and *deserving* of your help; if you accept that nothing you do is done without some kind of guidance from outside of you; if you practice on as many "guinea pigs" as you can find without charging them—well, then, you just can't help but become a really good reader! You can get to know nearly as much as I do one day, and maybe even eventually know all the stuff I don't.

See, what I've learned is that anybody with the determination to do all that stuff probably has a terrific talent for the tarot. All it might take is cultivation. In the same way a little green shoot is nurtured by rain and sun to become a big and beautiful plant, so too can you develop your talent and skills to become a fine reader.

In the end, though, the most important thing in that list is caring: caring about every client the same way you care about the people you love. Because if you're able to care that much, you'll probably work really hard to do the best job you can. And that heart connection, invisible though it is, is the secret to it all.

So like the ad says, just do it!

Miscellaneous Spreads

The Celtic Cross

As I mentioned earlier, when I started out as a reader, I used the Celtic Cross because it's the one in all the books. I discovered that this spread can provide an enormous amount of information, but it also takes a lot of time to comprehend. This just isn't good when your meter is running and your client isn't rich.

So I found a quicker way to get the same information: the seven-card spread that I've been stressing in this book.

Still, the Celtic Cross has stood the test of time, so here goes.

Traditionally, the placements of the cards in the Celtic Cross spread have the following meanings:

Card 1: The significator (a person, a Court Card, to symbolize the client; I *don't* use a significator)

Card 2: The client's present situation (what helps or opposes the client)

Card 3: Whatever is causing the current situation

Card 4: What underlies the current situation (what is at the root of things)

Card 5: What is just passing (*more on this in a minute*)

Card 6: The immediate future

Card 7: The subconscious

Card 8: The environment ("rules" card 7)

Card 9: What is feared/hoped; anxieties

Card 10: The outcome

These are the traditional meanings given for the placements of the cards using the Celtic Cross, but over the years I discovered something very useful: Card 5 is usually not about what is passing. It's usually about what will be passing just before the rest of the events in the spread begin. So card 5 has usually not happened yet. Which means you can almost time the situation to come based on what will happen first: card 5.

Also, I discovered that card 4 can act as a root. So if card 4 is the root, what is the rest of the tree? Say card 4 is a Pentacle card. Then the rest of the cards (the tree) are probably going to be addressing practical issues, first and foremost.

As for card 1, suppose you choose the Queen of Rods/Wands (a woman willing to make a commitment) for the significator for an Aries woman. If you choose to put this card down first, then it cannot fall anywhere else in the spread. And this Queen in the #10 spot—the outcome—would be a *great* thing. Or suppose in the #10 spot she would have fallen reversed (a woman *not* willing to make a commitment): this would've been crucial to know, right?

So, as I said, *I do not choose a significator,* not even for the Celtic Cross. I simply place the first card after shuffling in the #1 spot, and it becomes the issue at hand.

Also, I discovered that sometimes the last four cards are telling a *different* story than the first six cards. It's as if somebody has two issues running along on parallel tracks and both are equally important.

So you can see how this spread can be totally complicated and can turn something relatively simple into something way too hard.

Still, if you like the whole idea, there are books out there with far more information and guidance on the Celtic Cross. Even then, though, you'll need to add cards to the ten basic cards on the table if you want to get any kind of elaboration and clarity.

Here is a diagram of the Celtic Cross, with the order in which you lay down the cards. Card 2 is placed atop and across card 1 to form a small cross.

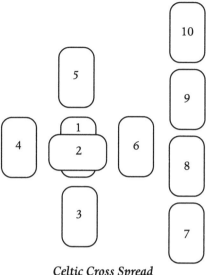

Celtic Cross Spread

Rune Spreads

Basically, when I have a simple question about something in my own life, I use runes.

Ralph Blum has done a good job of translating these twenty-five scratchy picture stones into usable concepts. (He says that when he got stuck doing this, he used the *I Ching*. Great!)

So if you want to substitute tarot cards for runes, you can check Blum's *The Book of Runes* for runic layouts and simply substitute cards for stones (though I don't).

What I Do for Me

Here I need to say something really important.

When I have a question about my own life, I choose *one* rune, *one* stone. And I ask this *one* question: "What is the best thing I can know about _____ right now?"

That's it.

I always get the answer I need, though I don't always get the answer I want. And I've learned to live with that. (And, no, it wasn't easy to master this acceptance.)

So I recommend that this be the *only* question you ever ask an oracle about your own life. Because we just can't orchestrate what will show up when we choose. See, we always get the right answers to the real issues, no matter how hard we try to avoid them.

A Spread Loosely Based on Astrology

If you're just starting out and you're like a kid in a candy store about this stuff, you may want to try this astrology spread. Personally, I've never used this spread with much satisfaction, I don't even know where I read about it. Maybe I just thought of it one day.

Basically, you use one card to address the issues of each of the twelve houses in an astrological chart:

First House: The self, the body, how the world sees us

Second House: Self-earned money, values

Third House: Siblings, short trips, and short communications; neighbors

Fourth House: The home, the parents' home, mother

Fifth House: Children, luck, speculation, creativity

Sixth House: Work and health

Seventh House: Relationships, partnerships

Eighth House: Death, rebirth, other people's money, sex, taxes, credit, psychology

Ninth House: Long-distance travel, philosophy, religion, government, spirituality

Tenth House: Career, ambitions

Eleventh House: Friends, organizations, groups, aspirations

Twelfth House: The subconscious, the unconscious, the undoing, "enemies"

(Please consult a good astrology text if you want the really broad meanings for each house.)

So what you do is to put twelve cards in a circle, counterclockwise, one for each house. Then try to understand how the cards you chose relate to the concepts given for each house.

Again, anything like this that makes your right brain work is fine. But I think you'll end up back at seven cards sooner rather than later, especially if you're working with clients. Like the Celtic Cross, this astrology spread takes a lot of time to do and interpret.

APPENDIX 2
THE MINOR ARCANA AT A GLANCE

CUPS	SWORDS	PENTACLES	RODS/WANDS
water	air	earth	fire
Scorpio	Libra	Virgo	Aries
Cancer	Aquarius	Taurus	Leo
Pisces	Gemini	Capricorn	Sagittarius
emotion	intellect	physicality	activity
love	thought	nurturing	talk/ideas
warmth	deciding	money	energy
friendship	asserting	values	drive
art	intellect	work	doing
receptiveness	strife	skill	loyalty
plumbing	nervous system	foundation	energy
water	electricity	structure	protein
kidneys	metals	skeleton	hair
urine	air	growths	immune system

CUPS	SWORDS	PENTACLES	RODS/WANDS
prostate	breathing	calcium	mental process
pipes	iron	food/vitamins	wood
summer	winter	autumn	spring

TAROT IN HISTORY

I have a theory that all oracles derive from one philosophical source that's been interpreted by the various cultures and styles of thinking to suit the abilities of the users.

For the religious, there are holy books.

For people who like math and science, there is astrology.

For the artistic type, there's the picture symbolism and color of tarot.

For the incredibly literate, there's the *I Ching*, which demands sophisticated reading comprehension and years of contemplation.

At this point I sometimes feel as if the secrets of the universe have been conveyed to this earth in all the ways needed by all the various peoples. There are scholars now who believe that six thousand years ago, ancient Sumeria was visited by extraterrestrials who mingled with the people there, creating "overnight" a cultural and philosophical revolution.

And from the TV program *Ancient Aliens*, I realized that the tarot symbolism of the Wheel of Fortune is suspiciously reminiscent of the description of the biblical Ezekiel's wheel.

Sure, it's all just theoretical, but from "crazy" theories have come all the most revolutionary discoveries and inventions in science.

CHOOSING A PSYCHIC

The fact is that so far, there's no official system in the United States for testing and licensing psychics and others who work in the field of the occult.

So how can we know that somebody we're going to trust actually deserves that trust?

In my own life, I would never see a doctor, lawyer, electrician, plumber, reader—anybody!—without some kind of *personal reference*, never mind a license.

And if I let somebody into my life, I want to be sure that person knows what she or he is doing.

So I think the best rule of thumb in the modern age is to try to learn the credentials of the folks you're dealing with. The internet provides so many choices. Too many, maybe. Various professionals advertise in subways and on lampposts … but who *are* they?

Social media can't be relied on for honest evaluations of professionals.

So we always need to ask: Who *is* this person doing all of this advertising and self-promotion? Where is the *proof* of competence? That's what we should be asking. Always.

And so far, the only way I know to have even half a chance of success is to work with people who come recommended by people we trust.

Right?

APPENDIX 5

THE AMAZING THING ABOUT ORACLES

After all the years I've been working as a psychic, I'm still astonished that anything can transcend the limits of space and time.

For example, maybe fifteen years ago I discovered that we live our lives in cycles of twenty-three years. I discovered that exactly every twenty-three years a seminal event occurs in our lives and marks the point at which we can set off (whether we're aware of it or not) on an entirely new voyage in life, in a totally new direction.

After a while I discovered two more things: One, the twenty-three-year cycle, as I call it, does not necessarily start at birth! Most of us come into being at some point *during* the cycle, not at the beginning. Two, I can find no astrological explanation for this cycle.

It took me a long while to see that this is because, for most of us, our *selves* don't start at birth.

Then I noticed some other things. The DNA helix, for example, is two strands of twenty-three. And I noticed that 99 percent of the time, when a good fiction writer talks about the length of something like a job or a marriage or a relationship, usually twenty-three (sometimes twenty-two) years is given as the length of the thing.

So I did some research and discovered this: the earth's slow wobble as it spins on its axis is called "precession." This top-like wobble is said to have a periodicity of somewhere around *23,000* years. This can't be an accident. Genetics, astrophysics, art—and all agree?

And so at that point I realized with a shock that what I found, I believe, is the life experience of the soul. If most of us enter this life at some point in a cycle that started *before* we were born, what else could it be?

Now, I don't know what huge impact this information can have on people, but I *do* know that when I see the card combination for this cycle, it means the person I'm reading has a chance to make a completely new start in life. It means the person I'm reading will no longer agree to settle for anything in life. It means that the person I'm reading, if in psychotherapy, can be a successful "graduate" when the current cycle ends.

It means the person I'm reading can basically be brand-new. It means the person I'm reading should start now to build a bridge to the new life that will be starting when the old cycle is over (maybe go to school, get some training, get a license, whatever is needed).

And, no, it doesn't mean that all of a sudden life will be perfect, but it does tell me that the person I'm reading probably won't want to settle anymore. Ever. About anything. Whatever fears had been the driving force will have been overcome.

What does this mean in practical terms? It means, for example, that a woman will leave a loveless marriage because she's no longer afraid of being alone in the world. She's discovered that there are worse things. And a man might leave a lousy job for a new career, this time something *he* wants to do with his life and not the idea of his parents.

It also always means that what we dreamed of as a little kid comes back into play at this time.

I once read for a man becoming CEO of a company. I saw that the end of the current cycle was close. Twenty-three years. I asked him what he'd dreamed of as a kid. He said he'd always wanted to be a bus driver. I asked him why. He said, "So people would follow me." And I said, "Well, if you're a CEO, now they will!"

This whole thing is astonishing, isn't it? And though not everybody gets the chance to start over, just plain start over, if I see the cycle and ask you, say, what happened in your life in 1987, there will always be a significant answer: a birth, death, divorce, major move, first job, first marriage, birth of first child, birth/ death of a sibling, first sexual experience, and so on.

How do I know the year? I subtract twenty-three from now or next year, depending on how I feel about what I see.

And if there isn't anything significant from twenty-three years back, I just go back forty-six years instead to find the seeds of the present. Why go back another twenty-three? Because the one other really important thing I've discovered with this cycle is that if we choose to do nothing when we really want to do *something*, it may be *another* twenty-three years before we get the chance again.

And way too many of us seem to have taken the do-nothing approach the first or even second time fate came calling.

Regardless of your age, if life can begin anew, go for it!

To Write to the Author

If you wish to contact the author or would like more information about this book, please write to the author in care of Llewellyn Worldwide Ltd. and we will forward your request. Both the author and the publisher appreciate hearing from you and learning of your enjoyment of this book and how it has helped you. Llewellyn Worldwide Ltd. cannot guarantee that every letter written to the author can be answered, but all will be forwarded. Please write to:

Jeannie Reed
⁒ Llewellyn Worldwide
2143 Wooddale Drive
Woodbury, MN 55125-2989
Please enclose a self-addressed stamped envelope for reply,
or $1.00 to cover costs. If outside the U.S.A., enclose
an international postal reply coupon.

Many of Llewellyn's authors have websites with additional information and resources. For more information, please visit our website at http://www.llewellyn.com.